Saturday's Child

DAPHNE ECONOMOU

# Saturday's Child
*A journey through an Indian childhood*

OCEANIDA

First edition: February 2007
Third edition: December 2017

© 2006, Daphne Economou. All rights reserved
Published by Oceanida - trademark of NIKI Ekdotiki SA
38, Dervenion St., 106 81 Athens, Greece, Tel. +30210.38.06.137
e-mail: info@oceanida.gr
www.oceanida.gr

Typeset & Layout: Oceanida
Printed and bound: NIKI Ekdotiki SA

ISBN 978-960-410-454-3

Distribution by NIKI Ekdotiki SA
110, Solonos St., 106 81 Athens, Greece, Tel. +30210.38.02.242
www.greekbooks.gr

*For my mother, in remembrance*

*There's rosemary, that's for remembrance...
there's rue for you, and here's some for me.*

　　　　　　*Hamlet*, Act IV, Scene V

## *Foreword*

Usually, when people send me a manuscript with a request for my opinion, I must confess that I skim through it so as to form a judgement as quickly as I can, but when Daphne Economou sent me the typescript of *Saturday's Child* I found myself reading every word of it right through to the end, for she writes wonderfully well, and the whole book is funny, touching, and richly evocative of a vanished universe. Her capacity to re-enter the world of childhood is remarkable, her feelings and insights so true and so fresh. For example, her understanding of the anguish of parting from people and places one loves is so acute as to make one weep, while her vivid recreation of wartime Madras and Ooty makes her book a valuable historical document. Ooty emerges as one of those magical words that can sum up the joys that a once loved place can bring, and which one spends the rest of one's life remembering and trying to re-evoke: Ooty provided "a lasting measure of happiness against which all subsequent summers could be contrasted and compared."

The crowning achievement of this fine book is its celebration of two themes of great human significance: love (for two people: her mother and her nanny) and the archetypal "journey and return". Her mother comes leaping from the page as a living personality: her elegance and social poise, her natural authority and practical efficiency, as well as her occasional explosions of rage, and what it was like to be the subject of her "obsessive, possessive love tempered by fear." The journey from India to Greece is seen from opposing perspectives: the author's (Odysseus's journey out) and her mother's (the return to Ithaca). Her presentation of these themes is masterly, and we owe her a debt of gratitude for sharing her intense experience of them with us so beautifully.

ANTHONY STEVENS
*Author, psychiatrist
and analytical psychotherapist*

# *Preface*

This is a story of childhood and of a child's perception of place and time. It is essentially about memory and the reaches of memory; the recovery of those vivid yet indefinable images that defy time and the backlog of experience and knowledge. It is a story that could not be invented, but which is only as real as a child's view of reality. The one unquestionable fact is that my Indian childhood ended abruptly when my mother and I returned to Greece.

We were in Madras, in Kodaikanal and Ootacamund and Madras again. Years were divided into hot weather, cold weather and hot weather again.

There were good times and bad times, beginnings and endings, meetings and partings, but home was always somewhere else.

The book's documentary aspects are drawn from hearsay, photographs, letters and my Greek grandfather's diaries, but again only to the extent that these too are relevant to my own memories of that unpredictable, unconditional time, when anything seemed possible. I have purposely not checked the accuracy of what I remember, nor attempted to analyse people and situations from hindsight or from an adult's point of view. There are many questions raised and left unanswered because there is only as much there as was there for me then, and this includes our long, unescorted and often dangerous journey back from India to Greece, while there was a war still going on, with extended and memorable stays in Jerusalem, Cairo and Alexandria.

It was a rite of passage towards an identity that was mine alone, but the memories are shared with my mother, as the keeping of my promise not to forget.

DAPHNE ECONOMOU
Athens, 2006

## Chapter One

How the soothsayer got into the room, nobody knows. Perhaps he was visiting Krishnamurti* who was having his appendix out next door. Anyway, there he was with my horoscope in his hand and with much head-wagging and hand-wringing he repeated over and again, "Saturday child, dearie me...far to go, dearie me...many obstacles, dearie me..."

The soothsayer, with his predictions of doom, was all you needed after what you had noted laconically in my baby-book as "a difficult birth".

Father shooed him out of the room, yelling, "Jao, jao silly man, upsetting Madam!" But his

---

* Indian philosopher and spiritual leader (1895-1986).

"dearie me's" could be heard all the way down the corridor and the harm was done.

My grandmother, who was quietly crocheting by your bedside, was unconvinced that the soothsayer should have been treated so disrespectfully. She was immersed in Hindu metaphysics and could discern tinted haloes around people's heads.

Meanwhile, my persistent wailing for not being in your womb any more distracted Krishnamurti's meditation and matron suggested politely that perhaps it was time for us all to go home. It was Grandmother who raised the most objections, because according to my highly cynical grandfather, apart from assisting at the first confinement of her beloved expatriate daughter, Grandmother's expectations of India also included a meeting with Mahatma Gandhi and the opportunity to sit at Krishnamurti's feet. Over the years Grandfather had managed to humour most of his wife's whims, as long as they did not embarrass him unduly, but sitting at Krishnamurti's feet, as he lay in bed with his appendix out, was taking her fanciful aspirations too far. Especially as this was not the first chance encounter between Master and would-be disciple.

A week before my retarded birth, Father had taken you and the grandparents for a drive in what passed in Madras as the cool of the day, in the fervent hope that the bumps in the road would induce me to put up an appearance before the much-awaited New Year's Eve Party at the Madras Club, which he did not wish to miss. Reaching the narrow bridge over the Adyar River, he brought the Humber to a screeching halt in order not to run over three Indian gentlemen who were walking slowly abreast over the bridge in deep conversation. "Krishnamurti," announced Grandmother from the back of the Humber. "Nonsense!" chorused Father and Grandfather in unison. "There are at least three hundred million Indian gentlemen walking over bridges in the cool of the day."

Unconvinced by such shaky male rationalisation and believing much more strongly in her own powers of telepathy, Grandmother repeated the revered name. The three Indian gentlemen, unaware that they were holding up the traffic, turned at the end of the bridge and began walking equally slowly back towards the stationary car. The one in the middle was Krishnamurti.

"Elephtheria meets K.M." Grandfather notes in his diary, and on leaving the nursing-home: "Elephtheria invited to K.M. lecture."

You were not well. I had made trouble for you from the start of our association. I was too big for you and my determination to be born had injured your "tail bone". There must be a more scientific and less animalistic term for the bottom end of the spine, but you always referred to it as your "tail bone". It plagued you all your life and although, of course, you never blamed me, it was, I suppose, partly the source of my guilt. Later when you would scold me for breaking a toy, I thought it might have something to do with my clumsy birth.

We went home. Home was 10, Commander-in-Chief Road. You had called our house Delphi.

It was there that I began to be me, as the world padded by on flat brown soles and grass whirled in the mowing machine. Flower petals drifted onto the floor and the heat came through the blinds striped and dotted through the mosquito net. Somebody thumped an iron on the veranda and the crows called a clamorous welcome.

Scents and sounds. My India. Place of birth: Madras, India. Parents: Greek. The paradoxes were all there from the start. The servants planted a pipal tree in the garden on the day I was born. It is still there.

My father, Themos (Lyki to his English friends) was Managing Director of the Madras branch of Ralli Brothers.* Father's surfaces were hard and ungiving and his voice was loud. You were soft and warm and concave and I fitted into your arms and belly and I still did not know where you ended and where I began. Together we were scent, touch and sound.

It seems there was a nurse somewhere, but she did not exist for me. Only you existed.

My grandparents stayed on for quite a while.

---

* British merchant firm established in 1818 in London by the Ralli brothers from the Greek island of Chios. In 1851 the company began operating in India, dealing in raw materials. Many Greeks were employed there.

A ball of pink wool left in a drawer, after she left, was Grandmother for me. Grandfather was a whiff of cigarette smoke, just a whiff. Friends gathered round. I was the burrahsahib's* first.

"Never mind," the head clerk wired my parents. "Better luck next time."

Rosie, the wife of Memas Harocopos, my father's colleague, took photographs and so did Peter Mayne.** You, wan and beautiful under a silk counterpane with Grandfather by your side. Father on the lawn, looking tall and handsome. Me in a pram with Grandmother knitting beside me. The servants arrayed all around.

In a letter to his cousin in Greece, Grandfather writes:

> Perhaps our children's children are a form of immortality. Here the Indians believe in reincarnation, that after death they are reborn as monkeys, snakes, elephants, different manifestations of

---

* Big boss – Anglo-Indian slang.
** The travel writer, Peter Mayne (1908-1979), worked briefly as an assistant in Ralli Brothers. He was unhappy as a businessman and at my mother's persuasion, my father allowed him to resign without a fuss.

creation. We Greeks, in ancient times were sometimes transformed into butterflies, narcissi, even raindrops... more ephemeral beings...

Grandfather and Grandmother delayed their trip to Delhi after they were invited to dinner at Government House. "Protocol demands our attendance," Grandfather notes, not without pride. Finally they left on the train and "by some devilish coincidence," according to Grandfather, "who should be travelling to Delhi on the same train, but Mahatma Gandhi! Elephtheria overjoyed... I managed to get a snapshot."

Grandfather was never a great photographer. The extraordinary photograph shows Grandmother and Gandhi arm in arm, with the tops of their heads cut off. Just chins, torsos and bandy legs. "Elephtheria's claim to sainthood," Grandfather has written on the back of the photograph which he sent with a letter to the same favourite cousin in Greece:

> I managed to talk to him for a few minutes. Terribly shrewd, with wily little eyes and not a tooth in his mouth. He travels third class and at each station crowds gather to greet him... and

to give him money... he stretches his hand out of the window and collects alms for the charitable institutions that he maintains. Elephtheria is in seventh heaven and who knows, perhaps with the passing of time this photograph may constitute a claim to sainthood for her, if Gandhi is proclaimed a prophet by six hundred million Indians and worshipped as a second Moses or Christ or Mohammed! Keep the photograph, dear cousin, for your descendants.

They returned a bit exhausted, but elated from their journey north. Always interested in politics, Grandfather writes:

The British have granted all the Indians, men and women, the right to vote. Perhaps to encourage them to fight each other instead of fighting the British... but the poverty is devastating...

One day they were gone, to continue their trip around the world on the *Empress of Britain*. No more clicking knitting-needles, no more whiff of cigarette smoke... just the thump thump of Ayah's* iron on the veranda.

Temperatures over 110. Prickly heat. Up to

---

* Indian nurse and lady's maid.

the hills. Cool, cool and the scent of eucalyptus and mimosa. I had you all to myself. *Stopped crying, doing well.* Hands. Your cool fingers against my cheek and my hand clutching your thumb. So safe. *Starts to smile.*

New sounds and colours. My eyes were no longer dazzled by the glare of tropical light and I knew the crunch of your feet on the gravel. Blues and greens, dappled and diffused. *Looks around – recognises faces...* One face, your face, and one overwhelming feeling, my love for you.

This is who I was. The one who loved you, totally, desperately, as you loved me. We were good at loving, you and I. You wrote blissfully from the hills to an old friend and a cousin of my father's in Athens:*

> The world is beautiful but sad – but most of all it is beautiful and its sadness is one of its greatest beauties. I have discovered that marriage is the wisest of human discoveries. Marry, my dear cousin, and you will discover the joy of sharing, the great beauty of small and ordinary things.

---

* The writer, George Theotokas.

When you find someone to love, you will tell her that no life is wasted, no error unresolved, and no sorrow that cannot be forgotten. Do I need to tell you that I am happy?

We came down to the plains. You and me on the beach – you in a headscarf and high heels, me stark naked, flat on my tummy or stuck in the feet-washing bucket. Rosie and Peter snapping away.

My first birthday, in a high chair decorated with flowers and a huge garland of marigolds. The servants beaming all around. "Missie Baba big girl now – Mummy and Daddy soon baby boy." Where was the soothsayer to tell them there was only going to be me? The crows sang "Happy Birthday" tenor and bass.

Home leave. A month on the steamer, four months in Greece and back again by sea. New home was Athens. Beeswax and shade in the great house, wisteria and jasmine in the garden. New sounding words, softer, lighter... and Miss Hardy.

Nelly Hardy was Nanny. She smelt of lavender water and Lux soap and her voice lilted between speech and song. *Funny girl... my funny girl... ba ba black sheep...* She was a Norton Nanny, in her starched uniform, but she was a Yorkshire lassie most of all. She had been in Simla "with a family" and in Athens "with the twins". She talked about them, but she loved me best of all, because I made her laugh when I put my arms around her and called her "Nelly". Sometimes she laughed so much she cried and that set me off laughing and crying too.

In Athens, Grandmother reigned supreme and you became the daughter of the house again – delightful, sought after, your father's daughter.

You were born in the seaport of Patras in the Peloponnese, to a brilliant self-made man and the most beautiful woman of her day. You grew up with your two adored brothers and a devoted German Fraulein, in the famous house on the Square of the High Threshing Fields, with the twelve terracotta gods of Olympus on the rooftop, until the troubles began. Your father had made a fortune in the currant trade, but the overwhelming passion of his life was Elephtherios Venizelos, the great liberal politician.

As children, you and your brothers were caught up in the storm of political events that tore the country apart. Fleeing to Corfu in the middle of the night.* *Can I wear my fur muff, Mother? I want Fraulein, Mother... I want Fraulein...* They never told you she had died of typhoid fever, only that she had gone away... *How could she go without saying goodbye... I thought she loved me... When are we going back to Patras, Mother... We never said goodbye... Sometime darling.*

You never went back. You never said goodbye. You caught the terror of sudden partings then. It haunted you all your life.

Your father became Minister of National Economy in the Venizelos Government and the family moved to Athens, to the beautiful shady house on Tsakalof Street. But your heart remained in Patras forever.

Grandmother had golden hands that made golden sounds. The cluck-cluck of the wooden

---

* Many Venizelist families fled into exile in 1917, when the British blockaded Athens and Venizelos formed a second government in Salonica.

bobbins, the click-click of the steel knitting needles and best of all, the jug-jug of the silver spoon against the crystal glass, as she beat egg yolks with sugar for Grandfather's breakfast. Grandmother smelt of vanilla.

Nanny Hardy had a song for every occasion and there were so many people she knew. Jack and Jill, Little Tommy Tucker, Tom Tom the Piper's Son, Little Boy Blue, Mary Mary. "But *you*, little girl," she would say, "are sugar and spice."

Bad things happened in Nanny's songs ...*He had a great fall... he broke his crown... the cradle did fall... he went howling down the street... Johnny's so long at the fair...*

"But *you* little girl are everything nice." She made me feel safe.

My first concrete memory, which was more than hands and faces and sounds and smells, was the big earthquake. The cupboard in our room rocked backwards and forwards and we all went down into the garden in the middle of the night. I was not afraid because you and Nanny were there and Grandmother made it seem like a party. "Our girl is never afraid,"

Nanny said proudly, holding me in her arms all the same.

My second memory is the house smelling of incense and candle-wax, full of people and voices and noises. A big man with a beard and a black hat like a kettle on his head, put his dirty oily fingers on my forehead.

It seems that Grandmother had some idea that I hadn't been properly baptised by the Anglican priest in Madras and asked the priest who was christening my cousins to bless me too! Before the christening we were all three scrubbed in the washhouse by the washerwoman, standing naked on the marble slab where she scrubbed the clothes. Green soap and vinegar to make our hair shine.

My last memory of Greece is being jumped from chair to chair and somebody, perhaps me, crying in the great hall of Grandmother's house...

"When was it, Mother?"

"The day we left to return to India."

## Chapter Two

The sea voyage back to India from Greece took almost two months. I was sick on the steamer and my cot rolled up and down the cabin and bumped into the walls. The racehorses that were travelling with us put their heads out of their boxes and cried real tears. "Give them some sugar, darling."

Home in Madras again. Real birthplace home.

A new word everywhere. War. "What is war, Nanny?"

"Brave boys getting killed, darling." I see the faded picture of Tom in her apron pocket. "My Tom. He went to war and he never came home."

"Are girls killed, Nanny?"

"No, girls are nurses. They look after the wounded soldiers."

Something was badly wrong. Suddenly Mother left Madras to return to Europe.

"Why has Mother gone away?"

"You made her sick," Father said. So it was my fault after all.

At first there is a total blackout of memories. I only remember the nightmares. Mother on a cliff, way out over a precipice, reaching backwards to grasp my hand. "Help me darling... please help me..."

"I can't reach you Mother... I can't reach you..." Screaming in the night. Memories begin, but they are the wrong ones. I slip out of Nanny's hands covered in soap and run out onto the lawn, where Father has guests. My shadow running beside me terrifies me so, that I scream and fall down in the prickly grass. Father picks me up angrily. He writes to you: "Are we sure that the child isn't wrong in the head?"

To put me right and toughen me up, he takes me to the beach with a couple of friends from the office and nearly drowns me. Somebody lets go of my hand and I am being scraped along the sand at the bottom of the sea with a mountain of waves over me. They are all in a panic, searching for me in the waves, but Father is angry again.

You and Grandmother go to Paris for the operation on your lower spine and get caught in the war. Warsaw has fallen and France and Britain have declared war on Germany.

"How do cities fall, Nanny?"

"Like *London Bridge is falling down*, darling."

Nanny has a rhyme for everything, but where are you, where is Mother? Nanny cherishes and loves me and I love her too, really I do, but my longing for you is like pain. "Missie Baba very sad," Sam says. Sam is our butler and he knows. "Please eat, Missie Baba." But I can't eat. Nothing will go down.

How you and Grandmother returned home became a family legend to be recalled and embellished over the years. Grandmother in hysterics, behaving like a madwoman, tearing up her documents. "We will be arrested as enemy aliens or spies!" You, still frail from the operation. Telegrams from Athens: *Return immediately.*

Paris in chaos, with people fleeing in all directions, except for the Spanish émigrés who were fleeing *into* Paris to escape the Civil War. No passage home. You appeal to Father's firm, the Greek and British Embassies, the Foreign Office, the Greek shipowners. "Quite impossible. You will have to stay for the duration," is all they can say. Grandmother weeping, "We have to get home! My family are in Athens and my daughter's husband and child are in India!" Grandfather wires: *Very worried. Try to reach London.* More wires from India: *Very anxious.* Perhaps Father was anxious about being stuck alone with me "for the duration".

Finally Grandmother manages to book a seat on the Simplon and arrives home. Stavros Niarchos* finds a way for you to reach London. You stay at the Ritz in style, but how to get home with no ships leaving? Again the firm, the Embassies, the Foreign Office, the Greek shipowners... not a hope. But George, the legendary head-porter of the Ritz, comes to the rescue.

---

* The Greek shipowner and a cousin by marriage.

"Leave it to me," he says, and there on your dressing table is a ticket on the last boat out. "Elephtheria home and Dora too," Grandfather writes laconically in his diary, hiding his relief.

You arrive in Madras on the train. I am at the station with Father and a huge bunch of flowers. You seem to be hanging out of the compartment with one hand, standing on the step and waving and waving. I drop the flowers and run. I hang round your neck so nobody else can even get close enough to greet you.

At Delphi, Sam and Ayah beaming, and all the servants lined up to welcome you, with lemons for luck and garlands of marigolds. The house feels like home again. Father is happy too.

We go up to the hills, to Kodaikanal, you and I and Nanny and half the servants. Our house is called Downlands. It smells of wood smoke and kerosene oil. There is no electricity or running water. The kerosene lamps stand on a shelf in the kitchen and are lit and distributed to each room when it starts getting dark; the water-boy fills the tin tubs and washbasins with hot and cold water, and the sweeper creeps in like a shadow and empties the thunderboxes* when nobody is looking. I loved it, even though the jackals barked and the hyenas laughed all night, but you always said, "That house never wanted us." Though I think that must have been when everything started to go wrong, the second year.

The first year, Nanny started a chicken farm at Downlands by mistake. The cook bought a live hen from the bazaar for lunch and was about to chop off its head, when from fright I suppose, she laid an egg.

"We can't eat a laying hen," Nanny announced and ordered Chokra** to rig up a hencoop, where the hen was ensconced in style. You called her Antoinette, for reasons then not clear to me. Next day Nanny said Antoinette looked lonely, so we bought Snow White and a couple of others to keep her company. Prince Charming arrived all fuss and bother a week later, and then the yellow balls of chicks began. They all

---

\* Lavatory chamber pots.
\*\* Houseboy.

scampered and tweeped merrily in the coop. But one night a jackal got Snow White. All we found were her feathers.

"This will not do at all," Nanny said. "Make a wish darling." My wish sounded a bit odd. "Jackal no eat chicken." But the next day Ashie arrived. "That's a 'Saturday child' for you," Nanny said. "Her wishes come true." Ashie was a stray sheep dog and he set himself up to guard our chickens. He recruited his friend Patchy and they took it in turns every night. The word soon got around to the jackals, except one night when Cook left the door open and one of the hens got out of the pen.

I was in the tin tub in the middle of my room, having my bath. Suddenly there was a commotion outside and in through the window flew a terrified hen, hotly pursued by the jackal, who was hotly pursued by Ashie and Patchy, who had just come on duty. Then came the servants all flapping and yelling and Nanny brought up the rear. The chicken, jackal, dogs, servants and Nanny circled the bathtub twice before the chicken found a way out through another window followed by the jackal, dogs, servants and Nanny. I shouted with delight. The hen survived and "learnt her lesson" and Ashie and Patchy received medals for valour. By the end of the hot weather, we had twenty hens. "All good layers," Nanny said.

In the mornings I climbed into your bed by the window and you sang to me. The old German songs that your beloved lost Fraulein sang to you when you were a little girl. Sad songs about soldiers dying in the Great War.

> *Morgenrot, morgenrot*
> *leuchtest mir zum frühen Tod*
> *bald wird die trompete blasen*
> *dann muß ich mein Leben lassen*
> *Ich und mancher Kamerad.*\*

The day before you died, sixty years later, there was a red dawn and I sang *Morgenrot* to you, so

---

\* Dawn, dawn
  You light up my untimely death
  Soon the trumpet will sound
  For me to leave this life
  I and my many comrades.
        Wilhelm Hauff, 1824

that you knew that even your Fraulein had come back and was there with you.

I had a Pierrot doll and a small bear dressed in a sailor suit. You sang *Au Clair de la Lune* and we put the bear outside the window and when he knocked Pierrot would not let him in. This made me cry even more than for all the soldiers dying in the War. I never cried from hurt, only from sadness, but this was a good feeling – so good that I asked you to sing *Au Clair de la Lune* every morning, so I could weep happily from sadness.

Paris "fell" while we were in Kodaikanal and you and Nanny were so sad. Sam didn't know where Paris was, so it made no difference to him, or to me, but I tried to be good for a couple of days, because I could always tell when you were sad.

Nanny took me for walks and we sometimes took Ashie on a leash. "Mind the cowpats, darling." There was one place I did not like, because there was a precipice and I felt that a hand was pushing me towards the edge. Perhaps I could fly... but perhaps not...

From the edge of the precipice, the plain far

below looked like Nanny's patchwork bed cover, and some holy men with dirty unbrushed hair sat with their legs over the edge, mumbling prayers, as the sun went down.

"Why, Nanny?"

"They're Hindus darling."

"Am I a Hindu?"

"No darling, you're Christian. Christians believe in Christ."

"How can I believe in Christ, when I don't even know him?"

"Oh dear," Nanny said, "time we went to church."

So we went the next Sunday, with me all dolled up in a smocked frock and matching knickers and socks. I liked the singing but the words made no sense. *There is a green hill far away without a city wall.* Why *should* a green hill have a city wall?

I decided not to ask Nanny, who was looking solemn, singing away, and I battled with that "city wall" for years. It was Easter and the priest told us about the crown of thorns on Jesus' head.

"Miss Hardy!" Sam cried next day, "Missie Baba is chopping off the thorns on the rose bush!"

"Why are you hurting the roses, darling?"

"For hurting Jesus." It was the least I could do for Him.

We went for a walk on the downs and we made a miracle, Nanny and I. It had been raining and suddenly there we were, Nanny in her starched veil and me in my mackintosh, hugely reflected against the sky.

Father came up to see us, and his hard surfaces and loud voice shattered some of our harmony. I could see sparks in the air. The servants became nervous and Ashie had his tail between his legs. "Idiots!" "Bloody dog!" Nanny and I stayed in the nursery most of the time or I retreated to the hayloft, which was my hideaway, and disappeared. "Where *is* that child!"

You were nervous too. It was partly the bad news from home (so many homes) and something called the Blitz in London, but it was certainly not just that. There was no room for me in your bed in the mornings, because Father was there in his silk pyjamas and hard back and cold heels.

"Sahib, I have a thought..."

"For God's sake stop thinking, Chokra!"

"And where *is* that child?"

Hiding in the hayloft, away from the sparks that were making everything not right.

"Why aren't you eating? There are poor children who have nothing to eat..."

I have a knot in my stomach again... nothing will go down. I wish the poor children would come and eat my food. I go into the kitchen, which is not allowed, and Sam gives me the curry and rice he is eating with his fingers. Little balls of rice. "Eat Missie Baba, eat..."

"Are you on a hunger strike like Gandhi?" Father asks next day, laughing uproariously at his own, for me, meaningless joke. Who is this Gandhi, I wonder, and what does he know about me?

In the hayloft, I talk to Tim. Tim is my make-believe friend and he understands many things that I don't. He is always there when I need him, but he goes away if I want to be alone. I am never lonely when I am alone, only when there are the wrong people around.

"Have another one, Mrs. L," Nanny says, "for

our girl to have a brother or sister to play with." You look sad and I want to tell you that I don't need a brother or a sister.

"Time to go home," Father says. "Enough of this running wild..."

I could never be good for love. I never got the knack of it, perhaps because I knew you loved me even when I was bad. With Father, it was different. I never knew if he loved me, so it made no difference if I was good or bad.

"Why do we have to leave?"

"We'll come back next year."

"When is next year?"

I have no sense of time beyond yesterday and tomorrow...but next year seems further away than tomorrow.

Tim says he will wait for me, but it is hard to explain to Ashie and Patchy. I hug them both and they lick my face and give me a couple of fleas as a souvenir.

There are trunks in the hall and a lot of running and shouting. I stay in the hayloft, especially when the trouble with the chickens begins. Nanny announces that the chickens are coming to

Madras with us. Some of the hens are broody. She could be very firm.

Father says, "All those bloody chickens – I'm not travelling with all those bloody chickens!" Cook is ordered to "dispose" of them. You are white and silent and that makes me so furious that I stamp on Father's foot and he slaps me across the face. I scream and yell.

"Let's not make a scene now, darling," Nanny begs. I *will* make a scene, whatever that is, if it helps to stop you looking so frightened. Father stomps out of "this bloody madhouse", Cook pretends not to have heard the order, you get some colour back in your cheeks, and Nanny says that of course the chickens are coming to Madras.

As usual, Father takes it out on Sam and poor Chokra, but he knows he is beaten. Next day he takes Driver and Sam and the Humber and leaves for the plains. There is no more buzzing or sparks in the air and I eat a huge helping of shepherd's pie. You smile and laugh and Nanny says something about "men" but I know that this does not apply to her Tom.

Getting all the chickens on the train was quite an operation. There were twenty of them in all by now, counting the chicks. Cook fetched baskets from the bazaar and Nanny packed them in with "plenty of air and feed". The broody hens had soft straw so their eggs wouldn't break and their bottoms wouldn't get sore.

We arrived at the station like a travelling circus, you in navy blue "for travelling", Nanny in full uniform and me in my camelhair soldier coat and walking shoes. Ashie and Patchy were lodged with an old lady who stayed in Kodaikanal all the year round. Chokra's confidence revived after Father and Sam left and he was full of "thoughts". Cook was put in charge of the chickens. There were trunks and bedrolls and bundles and baskets all to be put on the train. The broody hens travelled first-class in our compartment, in the washbasin on the straw, so Nanny could keep an eye on them. The waterboy, who was a local servant, stood on the platform with a woollen muffler round his neck and wept. He too had no sense of "next year" and was sure he would never see us again.

The train chugged off and Nanny made everything shipshape for us and the hens. Very soon there was a strong henny smell, which you tried to camouflage by spraying perfume over everything – also a lot of droppings and feathers. "Natural stuff," Nanny said.

By next morning the eggs had hatched and there were six yellow chicks scampering around in the compartment too.

## Chapter Three

Father sent Driver in the Humber to meet us at the Madras station. He didn't come himself. We went in the Humber with the hens and chicks, and everybody and everything else came in an assortment of rickshaws. The heat hit us in the face and the sticky dampness got between our necks and collars and ran down our backbones, even though we had all changed into summer dresses on the train.

"Drink a lot of water," Nanny said.

For a Norton Nanny with "principles" (another mysterious word) she was not at all fussy. But water was her one mania. "At least two gallons a day in the tropics." All boiled in the nursery on her own primus burner. "Can't trust the servants to keep it on the boil for twenty minutes." She was a great boiler when I was very small. "You'll end up boiling Chokra," Father said, which was one of those terrifying jokes of his that I invariably took literally, so much so, that I watched Chokra daily to see whether he had begun to look like a boiled chicken. Nanny didn't go that far, but she did inspect Chokra's fingernails every morning when he brought in the chota hasri.*

In Madras everyone was talking about the war, even more than the races. As if Hitler wasn't bad enough, somebody called Mussolini had attacked Greece. At 9 a.m. and 6 p.m. every day, Father ordered me to stop chattering and jumping about. That meant that he was going to give the radio, that smelt of hot cloth, great big thumps to stop it from crackling, and then he would twiddle the knobs until it went *pip pip pip* and sang that soppy nursery rhyme tune, *Lero, lero, Lilliburlero...*\*\* and started

---

\* Early morning breakfast.
\*\* The tune of *Lilliburlero* was adopted by the British Broadcasting Corporation's World War II programme *Into Battle* and subsequently became the identity signal of the BBC World Service.

jabbering away in a tinny voice, with everyone crowding around and pretending to understand what it was saying. Only you had an anxious crease between your eyebrows. "Anything about Greece?" you asked. Both your brothers had gone to war (like Nanny's Tom who never came back) and there was no news from Grandfather at all. Usually halfway through its jabber, the radio lost its voice and all the thumps in the world would not persuade it to go on talking about the war. I felt Father was not treating it right anyway. Thumping would not have got a word out of me! So it was war, war, war from morning till night.

"Say a prayer darling, for all the brave boys," Nanny said. The idea that boys are brave was nonsense anyway. I was much braver than my friend Basil, although it is braver to be brave when you're frightened than when, like me, you're not frightened at all.

Basil was my special friend and it wasn't his fault that Rosie held his hair back with a slide and his pants up with buttons. I never called him "cowardy cowardy custard" because Basil tried to be brave, but Rosie and Memas were so full of fears that he caught them like measles. With Rosie and Memas it was "no, no, no" all day long, whereas Nanny and you let me do all the wild things I wanted. Gradually I taught Basil to swing the swing really high over the treetops and to slide headfirst down the slide. Even to hang from the tree branch and ride the tricycle over the bumps. In the afternoons we had to stay in the nursery because of the heat, and once we took all our clothes off and painted spots on our bottoms, so Nanny would think we had measles. He was a good sport, Basil, and I always stuck up for him about the hair slide and buttons.

He was my first friend. We went to kindergarten, Basil and I. Church Park, run by Irish nuns. The first day we stayed outside on the swing talking, after all the other children had gone in. So far in our lives we had only been called in for meals and bath time. Sister Mary-Teresa came out to fetch us in. All the sisters were called Mary-something. At first, I tried to be good, but after a week it was too much effort. I threw a piece of chalk out of the window and it hit Sister

Mary-Louise on the bottom, as she was bending over to talk to a small child. She locked me in the bathroom. After a while, I got so bored, I turned on all the taps and was Moses in the Red Sea. The trouble with the Red Sea was that it got out under the door and ran all along the corridor and down the staircase, so that all the Marys were almost drowned like Pharaoh's army and they came wading and splashing with their habits up to their knees to get me out.

The nuns put on a Christmas play and in spite of the Moses episode, I was given a part. You were surprised, as I was still in disgrace, but Nanny said, "After all she *is* the burrahsahib's daughter."

There were actually two plays and I had to have two costumes. I took a chit home with instructions and the tailor was set to work on the veranda. In the first play I was a doll (the one with brown hair) and in the second I was a fairy. In the first play I wore my pink lace dress and I stood in a box next to a girl with yellow hair and waved to you and Nanny as you sat in the front row. When the toyshop keeper came in with a customer, he rocked us back and forth and we said "Mama". That was my first speaking role and I thought it was all a bit silly until Basil, who was a frog in the fairy play, came leapfrogging out onto the stage in the middle of the "Mama" scene with three nuns chasing behind him. That made it fun and all the parents laughed and clapped. I would have much preferred to be a frog than a doll or a fairy. The frogs had a great time jumping around and bumping into each other, whilst we had to wave our arms and stand on our toes and be altogether soppy.

That year, I took up drawing in a big way – but my repertoire was restricted to two subjects. One was a kind of squiggle, which I called a "swail".

"What's a swail, darling? Could it be a snail?"

"A swail is a swail."

"And what about the other picture?"

"Just an ordinary angel."

I drew swails and ordinary angels everywhere, in the sand, on the wall, on Father's newspaper. I was dreadfully repetitive. After the swails and angels it was people and horses. You told me about Joan of Arc in her red, patched dress. She was my first and lasting heroine and there she is incongruously on the title page of your copy of *Gone with the Wind*, patch and horse and all. You told me about Pegasus, so I drew horses with wings on any surface I could find, including Father's Annual General Report.

"Get that child away from my desk!"

My other discovery was words, wonderful words that danced in my head like stars. Magical words that sounded like music, even lovelier than the rhythmic jug-jug of the water pump, the drip-drip of the tap, the swish-swish of Ayah's sari, the jingle-jingle of Sweeper's glass bangles, the scratch-scratch of Mali's* twig broom and the tinkle-tinkle of the rickshaw bells.

"Hark hark the dogs do bark..." Nanny taught me to read. This was bliss. I missed out all the long words and read every book greedily ten times over. Afternoon rest was not such a hardship any more, because I could have my books in bed with me, with the fan whirling and the curtains swaying and the slats of the blinds half down.

---

* Gardener.

There was that wonderful aloneness that only an "only child" can have and which "only children" hanker after all their lives. There were places where I could be alone, when there was tension in the air, when Father was yelling at Sam for drinking his whisky, when you were scolding the washerman for bringing the washing back late, when Cook was yelling at the cook-boy in the kitchen, when Water-boy tried to kill his wife and the policeman came on his bicycle in his white topi* and uniform to arrest him. Whenever there was any trouble of this sort, I would hide in the linen cupboard or in the box-room under the stairs, not from fear, but just to be away from it all and alone.

At Christmas there was a party at the Adyar Club** for all the children. We sat on the lawn and watched Punch and Judy bashing each other over the head. The English nannies sat on chairs

---

\* Hard hat made of cork.
\*\* A club, by the Adyar River, in a beautiful 18th century mansion known as Moubray's Cupola. Unlike the Madras Club, the Adyar admitted the wives and children of members.

at the back, the Anglo-Indians on stools in the middle, and the ayahs squatted on the lawn.

Afterwards we had cucumber sandwiches and ice cream and lemonade and too many sick-making cakes and then Father Christmas turned up in a different way every year. Once he came on a white horse, the next time on the fire-engine with all the bells clanging, and the last year he came punting round the bend of the river, which was the most beautiful way to arrive. I was a bit afraid of his red face and long beard and loud voice and kept my distance, even when he started handing out presents. Also, there was something that reminded me of Brigadier Maitland, who had been to dinner at Delphi and mumbled, "well, well, well..." just like Father Christmas. It struck me as a boring thing to say.

You and Father went out every evening. In his book, *The Pagoda Tree*, Michael Malin* writes:

> There was a handful of Greeks in Chinnapatnam [his name for Madras], and they were clearly

---

* Michael Malin, *The Pagoda Tree*, Kenneth Mason Publication Ltd, London 1963.

rather *chic*; they tended to orbit in and about the GH* set...

You and Father broke out of the boxwallah** caste and were invited to Government House. You came down to kiss me goodnight in your beautiful evening dresses.

"You are so pretty, Mummy," and your perfume lingered after you were gone. Father was handsome too in his dinner jacket or tails and he told me funny stories, so we laughed together and that was the best kind of sharing. I didn't mind you going out when Nanny was there, but I minded on her day-out when Ayah was in charge of me. Ayah was very Christian and very old; Father called her Mary-Jesus because she was always talking to them. She sat on the floor and rocked backwards and forwards and whined and whined, and it made me so depressed that I wanted the night to pass quickly and the day to come.

On my next birthday there was a treat. We all went to the cinema to see *Snow White*. You and

---

\* Government House.
\*\* Merchant class (Anglo-Indian slang).

me and Nanny, Basil and Rosie and your friend Paula with her two children, Heather and Alexander. Alexander was so small that Paula sat him on her knee. That afternoon we all caught the chronic terror of a whole generation of children nurtured on Walt Disney's gothic fantasies. The trees with outstretched arm-like tendrils clutching, and the wicked witch shrieking up the pointed mountain, haunted us well into adulthood. Alexander whimpered in Paula's arms and Basil had his eyes shut tight and his head under the seat but, as usual, I sat bolt upright staring ahead, with my heart beating like a drum.

Three days later I sensed that something was badly wrong. There was a lot of worried-sounding whispering and when Dr. Appel appeared with a grim face to vaccinate us all, I knew without a doubt that there was some kind of hidden danger, some threat, much worse than stray dogs or barking jackals or even cobras that could be seen.

"What is it, Mother?"

"Alexander has caught smallpox."

Little Alexander, so afraid of the wicked witch.

"Perhaps the witch made him sick."

"Perhaps, my darling."

"Those crazy people," Nanny said, "living down by the port and not having their children vaccinated!"

Dr. Appel came again and revaccinated us all, because "we can't take any chances".

Paula was as beautiful as the lady in the big Michelangelo book, with Jesus dead, lying across her lap. I was bewitched by her beauty and when she performed stories for us, out of Hans Christian Andersen, playing all the parts, I was even more enchanted.

Nanny never appreciated Paula's acting.

"Silly woman, dancing in the dew," Nanny said. Heather was a sweet girl, her voice was low and she was kind and gentle, not rough and rowdy like me. She took me by the hand the first time we met, and all I wanted in the world was to have plaits tied with red ribbons like Heather.

Alexander was small and not really noticeable yet, but their father belonged to some weird cult and walked along the beach in a long white robe, whispering and mumbling strange, nonsensical words.

"You'll catch hookworm, walking barefoot like that," I told him the first time I met him. "That was not very polite," you said, but you were smiling, and Nanny said, "Our girl's quite right. Stupid man with all those *ideas*." It was because of his father's ideas that Alexander caught smallpox. He had taken his family to live by the sea, so he could walk barefoot on the beach at mumbling time, and he gave Heather ideas about what to eat and not to eat. "Shouldn't mix proteins with carbohydrates." "Nonsense," Nanny said, and Nanny knew. But the worst idea was that he never had his children vaccinated and now little Alexander with the golden curls had caught smallpox and might have given it to all of us in that stuffy cinema.

Snippets and shreds of information drifted through to the nursery from the servants' quarters. "The Sahib has left the house and run away and all the servants too... Memsahib Paula is alone with Alexander... the quarantine authorities have put a chalk-line all around the house and nobody can go in or out..."

One day, I was in the back garden on my

tricycle, when you came running round the back of the house and started climbing the iron fire-escape up to your room. I thought it was an extraordinary thing for you to do in your high heels and I ran after you, but you shouted, "Go away! Don't come near me!" Sam and Cook came out of the kitchen to see what the palaver was. They always loved a palaver, but they were even more amazed to see their memsahib on the fire-escape calling for Ayah to come upstairs immediately.

Through the nursery grapevine, we soon learnt what had happened. You had been to see Paula and had talked to her from outside the chalk-line, as she stood by the window. She was quite alone and Alexander was dying. You went in. You sat with her in the shaded room with Alexander there beside you in his cot, wrapped in cotton wool for the sores. You were the only one who visited Paula, ever, until Alexander died. "My feet just took me in..." you told Nanny.

Afterwards you realized that you might have brought the contagion with you and that we would all die, which is why for a moment you panicked and ran up the fire escape and had a bath with so much detol that all your skin came off. "You have a brave mother," Nanny said and I squeezed my eyes and fists so tight and held my breath so long for love of you, that I went all giddy and fell down in the gravel.

Alexander was the first death. Later our tailor died of TB. I caught whooping cough and coughed all day and all night and my temperature went up to 104 and my long hair made me so hot that you and Nanny decided to cut it short. I was in quarantine for weeks and weeks and even Basil couldn't come and play for fear of catching it too.

"Little Missie much cough," Sam said, holding the bowl for me to be sick in.

"Will I die, Nanny?"

"Certainly not darling! What an idea!"

"But Alexander died. And in the song it says, '...if the angels they take you, take you 'cause they're lonely...' Perhaps the angels are getting lonely..."

"Please stop giving the child those records, Mrs. L," Nanny said. "They're giving her ideas."

The gramophone was in the nursery and you

gave me all your records to play whilst I was in quarantine. The gramophone had to be wound up and the needle changed every time a record was played. Otherwise the song got slower and slower and the voice deeper and deeper until it petered out altogether. The needle sometimes scratched the records and then the singer got hiccups and sang the same word over and over, and some records had a bit broken at the top so the singer had to start in the middle. ...*between the moon and under the sun...*

I knew all the words and tunes by heart and can sing them still... *Night and Day... September in the Rain... When They Begin the Beguine... Old Man River... I was a Fool for Love... Smoke Gets in Your Eyes... As Time Goes By...* Your favourite line was, "When you pass me by, I get that old feeling". I was too young to have old feelings, but music and words were one more wonder of aloneness. I did not die, but by April the ferocious heat of Madras meant it was time to return to the hills.

"Our girl is looking decidedly seedy," Nanny said.

At least we didn't have to take the chickens back with us, because the mongoose got a couple and the rest had caught chicken plague and died. All except one, who was sent "to stay with Mali" according to Father, after we left. Somehow I was not interested in them any more.

## Chapter Four

The first night back in Downlands, the jackals and hyenas kicked up such a fuss and made such a din, as if they were welcoming us home. But something was wrong. You got thinner and thinner and the crease between your eyebrows was there all the time.

"The Germans have occupied Greece," Nanny explained, "and Mummy is worried about her people." We were completely cut off. No news was reaching us at all.

But there were good times too. I made new friends. I first saw the Dysons in a show P.M.* put on to raise money for the war effort. All the

---
* Phyllis-Mary.

children sang, "There was a little woman as I heard tell..." and there was P.M. in a long green coat, being the tailor "whose name was Stout". She had a huge pair of scissors and she cut the little woman's "petticoats all about" while Taddy stood on the stage with the children singing. I was totally bewitched and strangely excited by what, I suppose, are the sexual implications of the song. I spent even more time in the hayloft with Tim.

The Dysons became part of our life. There was P.M. and Taddy and Taddy's stepsister, Jo. Their father, Scrubby, was a doctor in the railways, but he was down in the plains. Taddy was "solid" and blond. Jo was "willowy" and red-haired. Taddy had a lovely smile. Jo had a lovely scowl. I practiced both in front of the mirror, but could not get either quite right.

"Don't wiggle the mirror, darling – it makes me quite sick."

Then just as things were settling down, the neighbour's dog bit you on the leg and you had to go down to the plains to have injections in your tummy, while Nanny inspected the dog every day to see if it was frothing at the mouth. Meanwhile Father came down with diphtheria, so you would have had to go anyway to look after him.

That's when the Hoopoo letters began. Hoopoo was a funny bird who knew all about me. It seems that Hoopoo sat on the big pipal tree in our garden at Delphi and gave you all our news. Sometimes he rode on the fan in your room and once he dipped his paintbrush in the colours of the rainbow and sent us a beautiful picture.

Hoopoo was good at telling tales, but I wondered if he told you that I was sad without you and that this was not a good sad feeling like *Au Clair de la Lune* or even the death of Little Nell.* This was the same old blackness that sat on my heart when you were not there and made me bad.

"Try and go out," you write to Nanny. "Try not to get lonely."

So Nanny invited some little girls to tea and I

---

* Charles Dickens: *The Old Curiosity Shop*.

behaved very badly. Somehow Hoopoo got to hear of this too.

"He won't come any more if you can't be good."

We went to a party. I wore my party dress and tried so hard to behave, especially as there was a little girl with a wreath of pink flowers in her hair who wasn't allowed to run about at all. "Heart condition," the nannies said. Forever after I associated wreaths of flowers with heart conditions. I still do.

If they had let us play our own games it would have been all right, but we were made to play silly games like "Ring-a-ring o' roses" and we were not allowed to even "all fall down" so as not to dirty our frocks!

I don't know what got into me. One day, I cut a hole in Nanny's dressing gown and I even kicked her on the shin so badly that it bled. She didn't scold me at all and she never told old Hoopoo, because she knew it had something to do with the sadness inside me. Instead she organised all the servants into a cricket team and we played cricket every afternoon in the garden with everybody flapping and yelling and Nanny bowling and cheering us on. That helped the sadness quite a lot, until it started getting dark.

Hoopoo had told you there was a panther prowling around so you write: "Lock up well and don't be frightened." He had been to Greece and brought us news from there: "The Italians tried to stop him, but he pecked them so badly that they were frightened and ran away..."

We read about Christopher Robin* and Nanny suggested that we say his prayer, but it didn't make sense to me to ask God to make Nanny "good" – just so it would rhyme with "hood". Nanny was good because she was grown up, whilst I was sometimes bad because I was so small. Smallness was a problem altogether – there were so many things I could not reach and I still found it easier to go up and down stairs on my bottom. My eyes were level with Nanny's blue belt and the rim of the kitchen table and the door handle was just out of reach.

---

* A. A. Milne: *When We Were Very Young*.

At last you wrote: "Father is much better and Dr. Appel says he can go to the office for a few hours next week, so I can come back very soon." The day you arrived, still thin and tired from the rabies injections and the heat in Madras, it seemed to me that the sun and the moon and the stars all came out together in Kodaikanal to greet you and welcome you home.

P.M. became your special friend and I played with Taddy. Taddy was not bad, but she was not a goodie-goodie either. We played make-believe games and she told me about Bonnie Prince Charlie, who was almost as brave as Joan of Arc. Taddy was Charlie standing upright on the sofa and I was Flora Macdonald rowing like mad to reach Skye,* before "our foes by the shore" caught up with us. It was fun, much more fun than the silly games organised at parties by other people's bossy nannies. P.M. brought along her friend Vivienne Young, who was so pretty I thought she might be an angel in disguise. You chatted

---

\* The Skye Boat Song: "...carry the lad that's born to be king over the sea to Skye..."

and smiled more and laughed and I watched you while pretending to play, and was happy for you.

After Greece, the Germans had attacked Russia, but the Russians were fighting back. I asked Sam, "Where is Russia?" "Far away." His ignorance reassured me for my own.

I still had the after-effects of whooping cough and I found it hard to sleep because of a prayer I had heard: "If by chance I do not wake, I pray you Lord, my soul to take." It was not one of Nanny's prayers, but I had picked it up somewhere. The result was, I tried not to sleep for fear of being "taken". I lay with my eyes glued open, staring into the dark, until you, sensing that something was wrong, would come and sit by me, easing me gently into sleep.

"Why didn't you say that it was that silly prayer that was frightening you?" you asked later. That was my problem all my life; I could never express certain fears, not from braveness, but because words would define them more clearly and render them more real.

We stayed in the hills longer than usual so we could all recuperate, but the nights were getting longer and colder and Cook insisted that he had seen a tiger's footprints in the garden, so down we all went again, to Madras.

Soon after we arrived, the Japanese attacked Pearl Harbour, and America and Germany were at war. Soldiers started to arrive in Madras. You sent me to a new kindergarten after all the trouble with the nuns at Church Park the previous year. "Perhaps a smaller school where supervision and discipline are easier," you said to Nanny. "Church Park is too crowded and the boys are so rough." You always stood up for me. Mrs. Higgins had a schoolroom in her home. "*Try* to be good darling, *please.*"

I did try because I liked Mrs. Higgins better than the nuns. She had a kind face, and her schoolroom was full of sunlight and bright colours. But I still seemed to end up in the corner most days. Finally Mrs. Higgins discontinued this form of punishment after I drew a swail on the wall. To encourage my artistic aspirations she gave me a piece of drawing paper instead. "What about a pretty house?" she suggested kindly. "Or some pretty flowers...? Look at the pretty flowers Sally has painted." Nobody ever appreciated my swails, but I settled down at Mrs. Higgins's, sort of.

You were wonderful with flowers. You planted seeds and snipped off the dried heads of flowers, with our aged Mali in his red loincloth and spindly legs pottering around behind you with an enormous watering can. You never got muddy or wet, but you produced a herbaceous border that was a blaze of colours, and the most lovely red and orange khana lilies, taller than me. And when the little nut tree that you planted failed to thrive, you said it needed sun and moved it to the other side of the house and tended it back to health. Entranced, I used to watch you moving gracefully around the lawn, calling all the flowers by their names.

The veranda outside my room was an extension of our life, where many things happened. Sitting cross-legged on his mat, with the wonderful whirling sound of the sewing machine and his short dry cough, the tailor sewed my sun-frocks with knickers to match, all edged with bias binding. Ayah ironed the linen and Father's silk pyjamas, with the great thumping iron full of live coals and the scent and sound of sizzling as it glided over the sprayed sheets.

A white stray mother-dog came up close to be fed at sundown, when nobody else was around, and the Chinese peddler spread all his wares, ribbons and laces and bobbins and threads, on the tiles of the veranda. And then there was the half-naked juggler with his juggling tricks. Stuffing his skinny wife all trussed up like a chicken into the flat basket. Sticking the sword through from end to end. "Madam go to Calcutta." Opening the basket and Madam has disappeared. Opening it again and out she pops with all the trussing gone. Then the mango pip in a pile of soil – the cloth over, the cloth off, and there is the prettiest little mango tree you ever saw. So far so good, but where things started to go wrong for me was the other flat basket with the cobra inside. To this day, the sound of a snake-pipe gives me shivers down my spine, and I cannot even look at the picture of a snake in a book.

The hooded black cobra with its flicking tongue

rises from the basket and sways to the music of the pipe. "Little Missie touch cobra," the snake charmer says with his honeyed voice. I keep my distance, with my back to the wall, but once, just once, I look directly into the cobra's evil eyes and the terror is there in dreams, still today.

❁

One of the fun things I shared with Father were the Ghindy flat races. That year, he started taking me with him on Saturday afternoons and while you drank tea in the enclosure with the other ladies, he and I would inspect the horses in the paddock and choose the one to back. When I chose a total outsider called William Bell because his name reminded me of William Tell, Father backed him and he came in first by four lengths. After that, Father always consulted me. "Real horse sense," his buddies said and asked me for tips. Years later, after you and I left India, Father would write and give me news of William Bell. "William Bell has retired," was the last I heard. Most of the other children ran around and played at the races, but I found the cry, "They're off!" and the thud of galloping hooves, and the last supreme effort of the finish, immensely exciting.

That year, I taught myself to swim, sort of, paddling like a puppy dog, puffing and blowing and drinking gallons of water. Everyone seemed to consider it a splendid achievement, but with the huge waves from the Bay of Bengal towering over our heads and the lifeguards on the lookout for sharks, so that we had to come out at the sight of a fin, you could hardly call it swimming.

"Sharks are such a menace," was the general understatement. "Over one hundred casualties last year." We saw the vicious-looking hammerheads that the fishermen brought in with the nets and someone had his leg bitten off on Marina Beach, just a few yards up from where we were sitting, and bled to death before the ambulance men arrived. After that we went to the Gymkhana Club swimming pool, where there were no sharks.

Diving was what I was really good at and once I got the knack, nothing could get me out of the pool until my fingers went crinkly and my lips bright blue. Taddy and Jo came to the Gymkhana too, and Basil was always somewhere around. You didn't swim much and Nanny wouldn't be "seen dead" in a bathing suit, but I watched you over the rim of the pool, so lovely and cool in your cornflower blue dresses.

That was the time when Father brought a bolt of cloth back from the warehouse and we were all in cornflower blue. You and Nanny had blouses and dresses, and I had sun-suits run up in an hour by the tailor on the veranda. Ayah had a cornflower sari and Chokra had a cornflower turban; even Mali had a cornflower loincloth and we all had cornflower curtains and bedspreads and tablecloths and napkins and shoe-bags. There are still some around.

The English and Indian soldiers played rugger on a field of mud, behind the Gymkhana Club. The Indians played barefoot and it was all very friendly with everybody on their face in the mud most of the time. Taddy and Basil and I and a couple of others tried to scrum, like they did, pushing and shoving until we all fell down.

"Such a little tomboy," Nanny remarked adoringly. Jo never scrummed; she was much too ladylike. She walked around and drank lemonade with the grown-ups. "A bit of a so-and-so," Nanny said.

## *Chapter Five*

Just before Christmas, a Greek destroyer called *Aetos* [Eagle] turned up unexpectedly in Madras harbour, to the delight of the Greek community who turned out in strength to entertain the officers and crew.

Commander Toumbas writes in his war diaries:

> The few Greeks of Ralli Brothers, with their managing director and his charming wife, welcomed us with unbelievable warmheartedness... They visited our ship and organised city tours and country excursions for all the crew. We were constantly cared for and entertained, with a wonderful reception on our last evening...

I remember Commander Toumbas well, a tiny little man with a kind face. At our home on their last evening in Madras, you hung a small gold medallion of the Virgin Mary around his neck. "For luck," you said.

He wore it all his life, and when his ship was cut in half by a mine in the Mediterranean two years later and he still managed to sail what was left of her and her crew back into Alexandria harbour, it was your medallion of the Virgin that kept him safe, he always said.

In February 1942, Singapore fell to the Japanese and the two great ships, the *Prince of Wales* and the *Repulse*, were sunk off the coast of Malaysia. For the first time, I saw Nanny really crying. "All those brave boys!" I put my arms around her and called her Nelly, but for once it didn't seem to comfort her. I even tried being drowned in the bathtub myself, holding my breath under the water to see how it felt. "I'll thank you not to be so silly," Nanny said.

Everyone was talking about the "Japs".

"Are they bad?"

"Very bad men," Cook said, rolling his eyes and rocking his head. "Eat little girls."

Cook always associated everything with food, but it was small comfort. I escaped to the linen cupboard. And then, as if the trouble with the Japs was not bad enough, Nanny did the craziest thing. She decided to get married!

It seems that she saw an announcement in the Madras Mail.

"Look at this, Mrs. L, there's a gentleman in Mysore in search of a wife!"

And there it was in plain writing:

*English gentleman (50) resident and employed in Mysore wishes to become acquainted with pleasant English matron with intention marriage.*

With the cut flowers you were preparing for the vase in the front hall still in your hand, you sat down beside Nanny, all giggly, on the sofa to read the announcement over and over again, as if to conjure up an image of the Mysore gentleman.

"Do you think it's an honourable proposal?"

"Surely yes. He's even put his name and address."

"Jack Stapleton. Sounds like a good enough name."

"Shall we answer it, just for fun, Mrs. L? But you'll have to write it for me. I would never know what to say."

Next question: "Do I qualify as a matron? Perhaps he wants somebody with a hat and pearls."

"I think he just wants somebody... a bit mature."

"Well I'm no spring chicken, that's for sure."

And you both nearly fell off the sofa for laughing. So you wrote a beautiful letter to the Mysore gentleman, on Nanny's behalf, and Jack Stapleton was hooked like a trout.

"How could you be so stupid!" Father shouted. "Fancy losing our Nanny in the middle of the war!"

"It is her last chance at happiness."

"Nonsense, she's perfectly happy with us... and much too old to marry. He's probably a regular lout, working in the gold mines... But naturally if you go and write her letters for her, what do you expect!"

So that was that. I heard nothing more until we went up to Kodaikanal and when I did hear bits of talk, it didn't really make any difference, because Nanny was there and nothing had changed.

But one day you said, "You know, Nanny will not be with us any more after she marries."

"What do you mean?"

"She will live in Mysore with Jack."

"She can't. She has to stay with me."

You tried again another day.

"You can be a bridesmaid at Nanny's wedding."

"She's not going to her wedding and neither am I."

"What about Jack?"

"I hate Jack. I hope he's killed in the war."

"He's too old to go to war."

"Then I hope he's torpedoed. And anyway, she loves Tom. So she can't love Jack."

"Tom never came back from the last war, darling. She can't wait for him forever."

"What is 'forever'?" Grown-ups were so unreasonable and so unreliable.

I didn't discuss it with Nanny at all, because I was so afraid that it might be true. But I noticed that her cheeks were rosier and that one day she put a little touch of perfume behind her ears and a little blue bow in her hair, which was a very unnannyish thing to do.

There was talk of a powder-blue suit. "I can hardly turn up like a blushing bride." But as there was no sign of Jack, I still hoped it was the grown-ups being silly as usual and that the whole marriage business would go away like a bad dream.

You were desperately worried about the situation in Greece. Grandfather writes in his diary:

> Our country's drama has reached its most tragic stage. The daily deaths from famine are no longer recorded and the hundreds of dead in the streets each day are carted off in handcarts. We are totally cut off from the rest of the world and from those we love.

Frantic for news, you sent a string of telegrams through the Red Cross, but nothing was getting through. Father didn't come up to the hills at all and that was part of the trouble, I think. "White trash...hot-weather women," I heard Nanny say mysteriously to another nanny. I had no idea what she was talking about, but I spent a lot of time in the hayloft with Tim, trying to work things out for myself.

Thankfully with the "Flap" at least there was no more talk of Nanny getting married. On April 16th, Grandfather writes in his diary: "Madras is being evacuated for fear of Japanese attack..." and sure enough, one morning the postman brought a telegram from Father in a yellow envelope. You sat on the wooden bench under the porch and opened and read it. Your hands were shaking. You were always afraid of bad news from Greece.

*Imminent Japanese invasion of India. Fleet departing from Singapore. Leave Kodaikanal immediately for Mysore.*

You sat there very still for a few minutes and then, as you so often did when something was wrong, you called me to sit beside you on the bench.

"Daddy says we have to leave because the Japs are coming."

"They can't come up here. They don't know the way."

"No, but we might be trapped."

This was the Flap. It went down in the annals of wartime India.

At first, the incessant commotion, the crosscurrents of running servants and the mountains of baggage was like an army in retreat, but you and Nanny soon got everything and everybody under control and the Flap became the first great adventure of my life. I could see that you were not a bit afraid, which made it all right for me. Within twenty-four hours everything was organised. The servants were sent down to Madras to be with their families, all except our beloved Driver who refused to go. "Never leave Memsahib and Missie... many bad men on road."

The greatest excitement was that the Dysons with Vivienne and her two children were coming too. Dear Memas, always solicitous, came over to see if there was anything he could do to help. He and Rosie had decided to defy Father for once in their lives and to stay on with Basil in Kodaikanal. A snoopy neighbour called Mrs. Mangrove dropped in by chance to see what was happening. "You're running!" she proclaimed in a voice like a train whistle. "Running!" It became a family joke.

We were not running, but we left the next morning. You locked the house and you said, "I don't believe we will be coming back." We never did.

All our belongings had been sent down to Madras on the train with Sam. All we had with us were our bedrolls, a picnic basket and two suitcases. Also an assortment of dolls and books for the road. You wore your navy blue slacks "for driving" and you and Driver took it in turns. Nanny and I were in the back and Taddy came with us to make room for P.M. and Jo and Vivienne and Pippa and Christopher in the second car. Christopher was still nursing. As we left Kodaikanal forever (you were right) Memas stood on the curb to bid us Godspeed. That's the kind of friend he was.

To reach Mysore we had to take a completely different route from any we had taken before. Driver asked instructions from various people in bullock carts, but after a couple of hours the local dialect had changed and he couldn't make himself understood at all. After that it was just a question of luck. On the only straight stretch of road, we lost one of the bedrolls and had to go back to collect it, but after that it was jungle jungle all the way. Real fairytale jungle with Mowgli and Baloo and Bagheera* and a whole family of deer leaping over the road in front of us. I knew that Bambi

---

* Characters from Rudyard Kipling's *Jungle Book*.

and Faline* would be there to greet us. It started getting dark and the trees leaned across the road to sleep in each other's arms. There was a full moon high in the sky and the car wheels still jumped and jerked over the ruts.

You craned your head over the windshield and strained your eyes to see in the dark, but the headlights only lit up a few yards ahead. I started feeling drowsy... "There must be a dak** bungalow somewhere..." Nanny said, between verses of *Bye, baby bunting...*

Finally a small, squat building loomed out of the dark and we all piled excitedly out of the cars. Nanny pushed open the door and went in to inspect the situation with her torch.

"It's absolutely filthy," she proclaimed, "and there are no kerosene lamps. We can't possibly stay here."

"Better sleep in car," Driver proposed. That's where he usually slept. The thermos flask was empty. Desperately thirsty, you headed for a

---

\* From Walt Disney's *Bambi*.
\*\* Travellers' bungalow.

bucket of rainwater on the porch. "For God's sake, Mrs. L," Nanny cried. "You'll catch typhoid for sure!"

We were all exhausted and caked in mud from a mixture of dust and sweat. The jungle night was so dark, with the trees blocking out the light of the moon, that it didn't seem like such a wonderful adventure after all. Suddenly Driver, who had been into the bushes to do something that he would never do in front of the ladies, came running back to say that he had seen a light. And once again there was a miracle. You and P.M. walked down the path towards the light with Driver in the lead with the torch.

When you reached a wooden gate, you had no idea what was behind it or if anyone would answer when you pulled the bell-rope, but the gate *did* open and there stood a charming American missionary lady saying, "My, My, where have *you* come from?"\*

So Driver came back to fetch the rest of us in the car and the missionary nurses were all there

---

\* There were American missionary hospitals all over Southern India, run by a remarkable woman, Mrs. Scada.

to greet us with enormous smiles. They took charge completely, clucking around like mother hens. You and P.M. and Vivienne and even Nanny were settled in large wicker chairs and given cups of tea (with something stronger in it). The baby was bathed and changed and put in Vivienne's arms to nurse and we all had hot baths and chicken noodle soup and were put to bed in cots on the veranda, with wonderfully cool, clean sheets, and the sky and the moon above and a falling star with a tail a million miles long. You came and sat by me and held my hand and it was bliss to lie there in the night, with the bright sky above and you beside me, totally safe. As I fell asleep, I could hear P.M. and Vivienne talking quietly in the dark, but you kept your hand in mine.

The story goes, that sometime in the middle of the night, you remembered that the steel box with the gold sovereigns that were to get us to South Africa, if an evacuation order came, was still in the unlocked boot of the Humber. But you were too tired to bother.

Next morning, there was breakfast for us all,

as the missionaries cooed around like turtledoves and sang: "Morning has broken like the first morning." I think we could have stayed there forever, but we had to move on. The box with the sovereigns was still in the boot.

We could see the missionary ladies in their long, white dresses, standing by the gate and waving, until we rounded the curb and they disappeared.

"Can we go back to the white ladies, Mother?"

"Sometime, sweetheart. Sometime."

The jungle gave way at last and very slowly and carefully, with hundreds of hairpin bends, we crept down the mountain towards Mysore. It started getting hot, and the dust pinched our eyes and tickled our necks and dried up our throats. The white ladies had provided us with plenty of boiled water and sandwiches wrapped in blue and white checked napkins and Driver could understand the dialect again, so we wouldn't get lost. I counted the milestones as we drove past. It was better than trying to read in the car, which made me sick. Mysore 100 miles, 99 miles, 98 miles... When we arrived at last,

Mysore was all marble and flowers, or so it seemed to me. Rhododendrons, oleanders, jacarandas, bougainvilleas, a blaze of colour, between marble balustrades and pillars and a royal blue sky. Like the pictures in my book of the *Arabian Nights*.

Our hotel was some kind of palace. A whole army of servants ran down the steps to greet us, resplendent in their turbans and long striped coats. What they thought of our bedraggled state I wonder, but they showed no sign of disapproval. The wide steps led to a reception hall that was larger than a football field and our room seemed twice the size of Downlands, with huge four-poster beds.

"Is there a pea under the mattress?" I asked. The great thing about you was that you always knew what I had in mind.

"Try it and see," you said, "so we know if you are a real princess or not."

You stayed in the bathtub for almost an hour to get all the mud off and the weariness out of your limbs and then it was my turn, with Nanny scrubbing and scrubbing until I was tingling all over and she was red in the face.

"What we need now is a good night's rest," you said, but just then there was a knock on the door, and in strode Father's nephew, George Draikis, whom Father had sent up-country "to grow up and get away from the girls". He was all dolled up in a white sharkskin suit, like an admiral. Father had commanded him to look after us and there he was, all spick and span, to "take the girls out on the town... Vivienne and P.M. too."

In your exhausted voice you said, "Good God, George, we're in no condition to go anywhere. We'll see you in the morning."

"Not even dinner? But Lyki said..." Nanny frog-marched poor George out of the room, sharkskin and all, and you just managed a wan,

"Thank you all the same..."

"Silly man," Nanny said.

After Cousin George was shooed out, we were all in bed and asleep in a minute. I certainly was. Next morning, typically of you and Nanny, everything was in order. How all our dresses got pressed and our shoes polished and the kettle on the boil, I don't know, but that's how it was with the two of you. "Can't lower our standards because of a small crisis," Nanny said.

And what about the Japs? Inexplicably and to the surprise and relief of even Grandfather in Greece, they set out from Singapore across the Bay of Bengal to invade India, and then they turned round and went back again. Father always said they turned back because they saw him guarding the Marina beach. He and some of the other men had volunteered for home-guard duty and occasionally patrolled the beach with their Tommy guns, scanning the horizon for the Japanese fleet. We never heard the end of how the Japs turned tail for fear of them. As Managing Director of Ralli Brothers in Madras, Father was made a kind of officer and received a medal for "bravery in the face of the enemy" after the war. Nobody took it very seriously. "A lot of bluff," Nanny said.

Cousin George was there in a dark blue bushshirt next morning and P.M. and Vivienne and Jo and Taddy and Pippa and Christopher all came down to breakfast, looking clean and rested.

I have one memory and one non-memory of Mysore.

The memory is the black baboon in the zoo. Cousin George suggested a visit to the zoo, and after the previous evening's unfriendly reception, nobody wanted to disagree. So off we all went. As we entered the gates of the zoo, we could hear a terrible yowling and howling. We asked the keeper and he told us that the black baboon's wife had just died and he was weeping and wailing for her. Perennially curious, I dragged you and Nanny over to the monkey cages, whilst the others went off to see the parrots.

And sure enough there was the black baboon, a head taller than me, standing by the railing of his cage, howling in misery. Before anyone could stop me, I put my hand through the bars to offer him a monkey-nut and wham! down came his great black hand and he had me firmly by the wrist. You had written in my baby-book, "Loves animals" but this was taking it too far. I screamed in terror, but there was no getting my wrist out of the baboon's grasp. He had stopped howling and was looking at me, quite kindly, with his great sad, yellow eyes. I screamed even louder. At last, the keeper came running and managed to unhinge the black fingers from my wrist. The baboon receded to the back of the cage and crouched with his head in his hands, rocking backwards and forwards like a miserable old man. He had not scratched me at all, but the pressure was so great that I had blue finger-marks round my wrist for days.

"Perhaps he thought you were his wife," George said, which Nanny considered "uncalled for".

My non-memory is when Nanny left to be married. I do not even know if I was at her wedding. I, who remembered everything since I was as small as Christopher, only knew that she was no longer there and that there was a deep darkness over everything, as if the sun had gone away from the sky. "Very sad," you write.

To make matters worse, all the others left for Madras (there was not going to be an invasion after all) whereas Father ordered you and me to go up to Ooty for the rest of the hot weather.

"He doesn't want us around."

I don't know if you actually said it or whether you only thought it, but I knew it was the truth. Of course I never asked, because again I was afraid of the words that would confirm my suspicions. I, who was never afraid, was always afraid of the power of words. Words could hurt so much more than any number of falls.

## Chapter Six

Ooty was all wrong from the start. Things had been wrong before, but this was the first time that you and I were out of harmony. It was not your fault or mine – it was the harmony itself that had been broken. You write: "Mummy coping well" but you were not. First, because you were my mother and not my nanny and the practicalities of nannyhood tired and bored you. Secondly, because I was angry and unhappy which made me disobedient and inconsiderate and thirdly, because you were angry and unhappy too, and I knew this, and I knew you were trying to be brave because of me and I wanted so much to help and comfort you, but I didn't know how.

We stayed in an ugly hotel where everything seemed brown, unless it was the brownness that had got into my heart that made it seem so. The walls were brown and the furniture was brown, even the tablecloths were brown. There was a brown ayah who was so slow in thinking and moving that in the end you did everything yourself, not in your easy, graceful way, but violently like a stone propelled from a sling. There was violence in the air and I was angry and afraid. I stopped eating and I broke your pearl necklace out of clumsiness and we had to search for the tiny pearls all over the floor. And people were dying all around. You took me for a silent, distracted walk and we had to stop for an Indian procession to pass by, with a lot of white-clad people and flowers. They were carrying a man who was sitting on a platform, with a wreath of white flowers on his head and a garland of marigolds round his neck. He was all white and floury and his head was lolling about.

"Why is he sitting up there?"

"Because he's dead."

"But he's sitting up."

"Perhaps he was a tailor, sitting cross-legged all his life. He's more comfortable that way."

*Grandmother, the most beautiful woman of her day.
Patras, 1905*

*With your two adored brothers and a devoted German Fraulein.
Corfu, 1915*

*Dora and Lyki,
the "chic Greeks"
of Madras. 1936*

*"Protocol demands
our attendance."
Grandfather and
Grandmother invited to
Government House.
Madras, 1936*

*The Greeks of Ralli Brothers Madras with Grandmother and Peter Mayne.
From left to right: Memas Harocopos, Rosie Harocopos Cynthia Cronopulos,
Alec Cronopulos, Peter Mayne, Grandmother, Dora, Lyki. New Year's Day, 1937*

*"Elephtheria's claim to sainthood."
Grandmother and Mahatma Gandhi arm in arm. 1937*

*You called our house Delphi*

*The servants arrayed all around. Madras, 1938*

*The shady house on Tsakalof Street. Athens, 1939*

*Nelly Hardy was Nanny. She smelt of lavender water and Lux soap and her voice lilted between speech and song. Athens, 1939*

*Stuck in the feet-washing bucket on Marina Beach. Madras, 1940*

*Our house was called Downlands. Kodaikanal, 1941*

*You and me in Kodaikanal. 1941*

*We sat on the lawn and watched
Punch and Judy bashing
each other over the head.
Adyar Club, Madras, 1942*

*Basil was my first friend*

*I could never be good for love.
I never got the knack of it*

Two days later, as I was looking out of the hotel's brown window, I saw a woman being carried out on a cot, wrapped in a white sheet like a bundle of washing. "The sweeper... she died."

"But she's lying down...she didn't lie down to sweep..."

"No, but they couldn't carry her away standing up...it's either sitting or lying..."

Death, death, either sitting or lying. I stood all the time, nothing would prevail on me to lie down.

Then plague broke out in the bazaar and the Indian quarters. The hotelkeeper found a brown rat dead on the doorstep of our brown hotel. "That's where the plague comes from, from the fleas on the rat..."

I was sure I would die from the plague. It was just a matter of time. They would put a wreath on my head and carry me away to some dark lonely place, far from you. I woke screaming in the night, haunted by terrifying nightmares and longing for Nanny who knew how to chase them away. But Nanny was gone. I never saw her again. My mind was buzzing all the time and there were spicks and specks in front of my eyes.

Voices seemed to come from far away and everything I touched broke. "What a dreadful child!" a lady with a dissatisfied look and a green hat, proclaimed through her nose. "So badly brought up." You were ashamed of me and I was no help to you at all in your sadness.

"Quite a social liability," you write.

I started to do mad things that I had planned beforehand. We went on a picnic with some people from the hotel who had "a nice little girl". Into the woods where there was a small, dark, bottomless lake. I did what I had decided to do. I took my most beloved doll by the leg and I threw her as far as I could into the lake so that she would drown. Everyone was shocked and you were hurt, because again you were ashamed of me. One of the fathers tried to fish my doll out with a pole, but she had sunk.

Then some wild woodmen started fighting and shouting and screaming and hitting each other with sticks. There was violence and folly everywhere and I wanted to die, to get away from it all, even from you, whom I loved more than my life, but not being clear about the wherewithal of dying I did not know how to go about it and finally decided against it. But the feeling of loss persisted, all that long, meaningless summer, and the fear of partings and endings. The need for things to last and continue, the need to keep things the way they are and to make things happen became part of what you called my "Capricorn character" but it seldom turned out that way.

At last, because of the plague I suppose, Father said we could come back to Madras. It was good to be home again and some of the sadness seemed further away, although it had not disappeared altogether. Father bought me a boy's bicycle with a bar. I learnt to ride it in a day, except for getting off. At first I fell off when I wanted to stop, but I got the knack in the end. I rode that bicycle obsessively round and round the house in the noonday sun.

"Please wear your topi," you pleaded.

"Mad dogs and Englishmen," Father remarked. The crazy things grown-ups said!

Meanwhile the Japs had gone and dropped a bomb into the harbour, probably by mistake, but it caused great excitement. Sandbags were piled outside Father's office and we dug a trench in the garden, which soon filled with scorpions so we never went near it, leave alone in it. But the real bother was that we were ordered to hang blackout over all the windows. It made the house sweltering at night and "it was so ugly" you said. I suspect that that was the main problem, because you only kept it up for a couple of weeks out of something called "civic duty". Then you started opening chinks and finally you stopped drawing the blackout curtains altogether.

Just before Christmas a policeman came by on his bicycle, saw our windows blazing light for all the Japs to see, and produced a summons for you to appear in court. So there you were in the Madras courthouse in your cornflower blue shirtwaist, among all the bazaar thieves. Father was too embarrassed to accompany you, but as usual, he press-ganged Memas to keep an eye on the proceedings. There was a long list of cases to be tried and by the time your turn came the judge was exhausted and wanting his lunch. It was incredibly hot and the fan had broken down. The policeman was there, faintly embarrassed, but determined to perform his duty and assist in the war effort.

"State your case," the judge ordered, mopping his brow with a towel.

"I ride bicycle in Commander-in-Chief Road..."

"State date and hour!"

"Ten o'clock, fifteen minutes, eighteen day December, Your Honour!"

"And what did you see?"

"Simply, see much much light from window... knock door... say no blackout... Memsahib make no motion... issue summons!"

All the bazaar thieves turned to look at you smiling sweetly at the judge, who had taken off his spectacles.

"Case postponed!" said the poor judge. "For December 25th!"

"Sir, sir!" cried the little clerk under the judge's desk. "Great Christian festival!"

"January 1st!"

"Sir, sir, great New Year festival!"

"January 6th!"

"Sir, sir, great Hindu festival!"

"January 12th!"

"Sir, sir, great Muslim festival!"

"Case dismissed," said the judge wearily. "Defendant acquitted of all charges. Two rupees fine."

All the bazaar thieves clapped their hands and that was the end of the ugly blackout that "clashed" you said, with the ice-blue walls of Delphi. Down it came and was never seen or heard of again.

But Father, for all his bravado, found himself in trouble with the authorities too. At a formal dinner party at the Madras Club, one of the "top brass" said, "Lyki, old chap, we're going to have to bring you in for questioning."

"What are you talking about, Jim?"

"Passing information to the enemy."

"Are you crazy!"

"We have it in writing, old chap. Picked up by the censor. Very serious stuff."

What had happened was, that a procedure whereby the Madras office regularly sent other Ralli Brothers departments, including the one in Tokyo, information concerning weather conditions in the subcontinent, had not been discontinued with the commencement of hostilities. One of the office clerks had religiously continued to stamp and post a monthly weather bulletin to Tokyo, with vital information concerning rains, tides, floods, winds, crops and other natural phenomena to the untold delight of the Japanese High Command who were intercepting every dispatch.

As "one of us" Father got off with a guffaw and a back-thump, whilst the poor clerk, "the blithering idiot" in Father's charitable terminology, received hell.

❀

On my sixth birthday, we had a roundabout on the lawn. Beautifully carved wooden horses with real saddles and reins. I chose mine, a handsome black stallion with red harness, and before the other children arrived, the coolies who turned the roundabout gave me a ride, on my own, with the riderless horses flying out all around me.

That year we acquired Tali. We had always

had a garden cat, a mangy sore-covered marmalade called Sousa, who slept on the veranda and was forbidden the house. But Tali was another matter altogether. Your friend Marie Buck, from the American Mission, brought her in a basket, after a couple of persuasive telephone calls. She was a beautiful Siamese, "a real aristocrat" you said, who immediately established herself in style on the peach-coloured sofa that showed up her blue eyes. She had an ugly cry and a snobbish disposition and would lie full length across the pantry entrance and claw at Sam's bare toes as he bore the dishes to the dining room. She produced her first litter of decidedly low-class kittens in Father's cupboard on the shelf with his silk pyjamas, leaving an unspeakable mess. Father condemned the kittens to death by drowning, an act of sacrilege against Mother Nature's creatures that had the servants in a state of religious panic and Tali wailing and searching like a lost soul.

She became a family fixture and would come in with my breakfast in the morning, tail in the air, meowing for her saucer of milk. Any attempt to persuade her to consider a more appropriate mate than the local alley cats proved unsuccessful. She chased one potential Siamese suitor called Nobby, kindly lent to us by Dr. Appel, up into the rafters, where he caught pneumonia and had to be sent home humiliated and rejected.

The next litter, all coal black, came in the linen cupboard for variation. All but one went in the drowning bucket again. "Cats can't count," you said and Tali certainly lavished a profusion of motherly love on her one and only.

The coming of Birdie brought balance and harmony to our domestic situation, which had been seriously threatened and disrupted by Nanny's marriage. Birdie never took Nanny's place and I was no longer confined to the nursery. I spent much more time with you and joined in most of your daytime activities, but Birdie of the white teeth and starched white dresses looked after me in an easy, unassuming way, so that you no longer needed "to cope" with me and could revert to your mother-role again. I could never love her in the passionate, primitive way that I had loved Nanny, but although she never became indispensable, she became an integral part of my life for the next two-and-a-half years.

Generally, tensions eased. There were less jagged edges. In spite of the war in Burma and the lack of news from Greece, you seemed more relaxed and Father's presence was more in accord with the bright and sparkling atmosphere you always created around you.

I learnt later what had happened, although no rumours penetrated the sanctuary of the nursery, and Sam and Driver, who must have known, were paragons of discretion. But their particular solicitude for you, their Memsahib, certainly betrayed where their loyalties and affections lay.

As Nanny had foreseen, Father had become involved with one of the women who stayed on in the plains, when other wives and children went up to the hills to avoid the heat and the early monsoon. You knew that this was not a mere flirtation, but when we returned from Ooty, the "person in question" had left Madras and there was at least an outward show of calm and concord that *did* drift into the nursery.

In the early evenings, before Father had his sundown* and changed for dinner, you and he would walk up and down the lawn, arm in arm, talking quietly and I would watch you from the big wicker chair and feel comforted and secure.

The war brought new friends to Madras and this, I believe, made a real difference to your life. You no longer had to conform to the rules of the ICS** officials and their snooty wives and you made friends of your own choice, who gravitated naturally towards you and remained your devoted friends for life.

Our home filled with enchanting young men, either stationed with their regiments in Madras, or on leave from the Burma front. Still "short for my age" I moved among boots and khaki trouser legs, and the masculine laughter on the lawn seemed to infiltrate every corner of the house. Some regiments had such romantic

---

\* In India, gentlemen had their first whisky the minute the sun went down.

\*\* Indian Civil Service.

names. Royal Scots, Black Watch, and even the more prosaic Tank Corps had connotations of conflict and heroism, where only the enemy ever got hurt.

Lucas Ralli, son of Father's big boss, was there with his beautiful low voice and pipe smoke. Ronnie Macdonald of the Black Watch, who had been ambushed with his company in the Burma jungle and left for dead and had walked alone through the jungle for seven days and nights, his wrist artery bound with a stick and a shoe lace to stop the bleeding. Malcolm MacAlpine of the Royal Scots, who had seen combat in Rangoon. Your special friend, gentle and brilliant Sydney Cuthbert, who never returned, and most of all and best of all, Giles Eyre, wonderful Giles with the great laugh, whom we all adored.

Giles became an indelible part of our life. You threw a party for his twenty-first birthday and his tales of misery at Winchester and his horrendous initial training were discussed and embroidered upon by Taddy and me, until he almost ranked with Bonnie Prince Charlie in our admiration.

With Birdie washing and ironing and starching and snipping obsessively, I escaped from the nursery and I think you enjoyed having me around. Our "boys" were there at every opportunity, even at breakfast time, and the house vibrated with fun and laughter.

## Chapter Seven

Sometimes when there was no cholera, we went to the bazaar, more for fun I believe, than to actually purchase anything. Driver kept a close, disapproving watch behind us and shooed away the beggars as we strolled hand in hand from stall to stall, pushing our way around the holy cows and trying not to tread in their hot steaming dung. I remember the clamour and the press of bodies, but also the mounds and scent of bright-coloured spices, black cloves, grey pepper, red chilli, yellow saffron. Also huge sacks of wheat and corn. From cupboard-like stalls: "Memsahib, only look, no buy..." Cigarette tins filled with garnets and moonstones, but also with rubies, diamonds, emeralds and sapphires.

"Little Missie, hold in hand..." There they were in my grubby palm, glimmering like stars.

"Can I keep just one, Mother?"

You bought me a couple of glass bangles for my wrists, instead.

At other times we went shopping at Spensers, where I was treated to large black and white bull's-eyes that barely fitted in my mouth and to the draper's shop with the great bales of cotton of every wonderful colour. "Not that awful purple, darling, surely!" And best of all was Higginbotham's bookshop, with the warm, soft smell of new paper that made me quite dizzy from delight. We visited the Little Flower Convent, where the nuns made exquisite embroideries for your evening gowns and smocks for my party dresses and where the little blind boy played the same scale on the piano over and over again.

In spite of our never-never-land existence, we could not get away from the war. The lights had gone out all over Europe, and in Burma the ruthless Japanese offensive had brought the line close to collapse and much nearer home. Trainloads of exhausted, wounded and sick soldiers began to arrive in Madras to convalesce. The malaria was the worst. They trembled from fever and the quinine made their eyes and faces and even their fingers yellow. This was a new face of war different from the "war effort" that had gone on before.

Before, all the ladies had knitted mile-long mufflers and were involved in the Victory Shop. The Greek wives had a stand, with a Parthenon-like frieze, where they sold home-made runny yoghurt and syrupy cakes. There had been a Grecian "tableau vivant" where all the ladies stood motionless on the staircase of Government House in a variety of uncomfortable and faintly ridiculous poses, all dressed exquisitely by you, in the second-choice saris of one of your many Indian friends.

Then there had been the War Appeal, where everyone vied with everyone else to raise money. Memas was dispatched to Madame Sophie, a Greek from Kalamata, who ran something called the "local house". Madame Sophie and all the girls greeted Memas most warmly and treated him to coffee and Turkish delight. Then Madame

Sophie walked solemnly towards the icon of the Virgin, crossed herself three times, unhung the icon from the wall to reveal a safe behind, crossed herself again, unlocked the safe and produced a bag of gold sovereigns which she gave to a jubilant Memas for "our boys". Of course everyone teased Memas unmercifully and I wondered what Father was laughing about, but nobody dared to doubt the success of his mission.

That was when the war seemed unreal and far away. Suddenly now it had become part of our own reality. American soldiers had started to arrive and the first episode one afternoon was when a huge, black, drunken soldier appeared on the veranda outside my room. Ayah kicked up an incredible palaver, squawking like a frightened chicken and brandishing the iron in his face to prevent him from coming right into the nursery. As the poor man swayed on his feet bewildered by Ayah's screeching and the unfamiliar surroundings, I stood waist-high before him until Father came down from his nap in his silk pyjamas.

Father bellowed, "What's going on!" and the

poor soldier saluted smartly and said, "Yes sir, yes sir!" whilst Sam frog-marched him out of the front gate, across Commander-in-Chief Road and back to his barracks that were just over the road. You said he must have turned left into our drive instead of right into the barracks and that he had probably mistaken Father with the brass buttons on his pyjamas for an admiral. For me, still battling with rights and lefts, it seemed an easy enough mistake to make, without necessarily being drunk.

Ayah's comments on the poor soldier's blackness seemed uncalled for, considering how black she was, but she went on and on about "the big black baboon with his dirty boots on my clean veranda" and how she had single-handedly confronted him and saved Little Missie from unspeakable dangers. Sam said, "If it wasn't for me..." but you said, "Let Ayah have her day."

One evening you took me with you to the Adyar Club where there was a reception for the "other ranks". The snooty Madras Club only invited the officers. It was not the noisy, tipsy occasion that everyone expected. Sick and exhausted, with their minds filled with death and atrocities, the soldiers sat on the riverbank in small groups, talking quietly or not at all. You were busy, so I ran around for a while until I sensed the inappropriateness of my behaviour in that sombre gathering.

As tropical nightfall plummeted down from the sky, without waiting for dusk, I approached a soldier who was sitting alone, apart from the others. He was trying to light his pipe, but his hands were trembling so from the ague that he could not hold the match steady and it kept going out. Standing, I was about level with his head as he sat on the grass. His eyes had that vague quinine-yellow look, but he noticed me standing there and said, "Will you give me a hand with this match, little one? I can't seem to manage."

I took the matchbox, lit the match and held it steady, as he puffed at his pipe. It glowed in the darkness. "Thanks," he said, and then as an afterthought, "Come and sit by me. I have a wee girl like you at home..." I was overwhelmed by his need of me. Then suddenly, down by the river, a group of black American soldiers began to sing one of those sad, faraway songs of slavery that tear at the heart. A deep bass voice picked up the tune, to be followed by a great harmonisation of wonderful sounds that filled the damp, warm, tropical night with longing.

> *Deep river*
> *My heart is over Jordan, Lord*
> *That's where I long to go.*

These are the memories of a lifetime, for which I am eternally grateful, of a time gone by, of my India.

❂

As the heat returned like a sledgehammer, Father decided to buy you a car so you could drive yourself in Ooty and he could keep the Humber and Driver in Madras. It seemed like a good idea and you were delighted. However, finding a car for sale was not the simplest proposition in wartime India. There were a couple of army jeeps in the depot and some ancient Fords in various compounds, but nothing suitable for a lady of your standing. As usual, Memas was put on the job, which he pursued with his customary zeal, and sure enough he soon discovered an Indian family willing to sell their Hillman. An appointment was set up and the Hillman, garlanded in marigolds, plus family, arrived. I remember a small grey car, out of which emerged a fat Indian gentleman, a beautifully sari-swathed, equally fat wife, followed by three children and grandmother who had to be unstuck and grappled out of the back seat. "Family car," announced the owner proudly, mopping his brow.

"Packed like sardines..." Father answered.

"Yes, yes, sardines...very good joke, ha ha." The car was there for all to see, the little there was of it, but Father made a great show of inspecting it, as if it was a racehorse. He poked at the grill in front, the way people who know look at horses' teeth. He stuck his head under the bonnet and peered in the engine. I wondered whether he would pick up the wheels one by one, like hooves. Of course it was all a show, as Father didn't know the first thing about the insides of cars.

After the inspection, the bargaining began. Foreseeing what was coming, you settled the grandmother politely in a deck chair with a lemonade and the two little girls at her feet, whilst Father and the Indian gentleman confronted each other on the lawn. The wife kept a safe distance. What was said and what the figures were I don't know, but Father's voice rose ominously, while the Indian gentleman mopped his brow more and more and slapped his son for no obvious reason at all.

The gist of the conversation was that Father said the car was "no good... scrap iron... lucky if anybody will take it off your hands..." while the Indian gentleman extolled its virtues in a shriller and shriller voice. But this time Father had underestimated the Indian gentleman's resilience or sense of pride and he had gone too far in his disparaging of the poor little garlanded Hillman.

Suddenly with a nod of his head, the gentleman ordered his family back into the car. Grandmother was squashed into the back, followed by the three children and Madam in the front. The owner then firmly shook Father's hand saying,

"The compliments of the season..." and seating himself in the driver's seat, honked the horn to herald his departure.

It was the first time I had ever seen Father genuinely disconcerted and you said, "Really Lyki! What do we do now?" The gentleman honked and honked as if to scare the crows, but as Sam would have said, he made "no motion" to move off.

"Call Memas!" Father pleaded, whilst trying to appease the gentleman through the window.

"You have insulted myself, my wife, my children and my mother-in-law!"

"No, no old chap..."

"You have also insulted my car!"

It was always Memas who saved every situation. Playing for time and encouraged by Sam, the doorman pretended that the front gate had jammed. The gentleman honked and mopped and distributed arbitrary slaps to all the occupants of the back seat, excepting grandmother, while you called Memas and begged him to come over immediately because Lyki had made a real mess of the negotiations. Sure enough, dear Memas appeared as if by chance, in his immaculate white suit and professed great personal interest in the Hillman. Out piled the family again and with many smiles and handshakes the Hillman was supposedly sold to Memas. Thus face was saved on all sides and you acquired a car. Rickshaws were summoned to bear the family away, with much friendly waving, and Driver drove the little grey Hillman ceremoniously into the garage as if it were a Rolls Royce at least.

P.M. gave dancing lessons to ladies and children in the Dyson's grand mansion with the black and white bull's-eye marble floors. You cried off because of your tailbone, but I was sent with Driver in the Humber twice a week. At Mrs. Higgins's dancing consisted of chugging around the room, being a train, but with P.M. it was serious stuff. P.M. played music on the gramophone and we all stood on our toes higher and higher... "keep your tummies in..." And then we ran around "lightly, lightly like fairies..." and we waved our arms "in the wind". Usually it was just Jo, Taddy and me. Jo was a beautiful fairy, although P.M. said, "Not so languid darling, and your hands not like bunches of bananas..." but to Taddy and me it was, "Fairies don't gallop, they float in the air..."

I don't think we were very good at floating and I couldn't help feeling a bit silly, but it was fun moving in time to the music and I practiced that a lot at home with my gramophone records. *When they begin the beguine...* float, float... *You must remember this...* waft, waft, *When you passed me by...* tip-toes and tummy in.

Jo was chosen to perform in the New Year's Eve play, before all the grown-ups. As General Maitland stomped out as the Old Year, Jo floated in as the New Year in a beautiful flame-coloured dress. Taddy and I were green with envy.

Father was in a good mood and my six years made me a more acceptable companion. Apart from my "horse sense" which won him bets at the races, our relationship was established on a common predilection for boisterous games and pranks. I was amused by his big manly laugh and joined him at throwing slippers at the crows that cawed in the window, even though it meant breaking half of your precious Meissen figurines. Once he threw a wicker chair out of an upstairs window to startle me as I stood on the lawn. You were not amused by any of this, particularly by all the breakages involved, and I am sure now that Father's pranks were aimed more at provoking and upsetting you than at entertaining me, but I was not aware of this at the time and joined in all his games with great enthusiasm.

Apart from the military men, couples and families arrived from the north and Madras became a hub of social activity. There were the Morlands, Bunny and Suzanne, with their two red-headed little boys, Michael and Miles. They were a sensational couple to look at and were labelled "great fun", a phrase that echoed the false gaiety of that precarious time. Everybody knew it was now or never, the foxtrot was all the rage and the song was *Anything Goes*. Nobody I have ever known looked as elegant in a morning coat and grey top hat as Bunny, but it was Suzanne with her delightful exuberance who made all the difference.

The arrival of Suzanne became one of the Madras legends. Bunny had come ahead and Suzanne wired that she was setting out from somewhere up north with the two boys, two bearers, two wolfhounds and fifteen trunks. At the appointed day and hour, Bunny went to the station to meet his family. The train arrived, but there was no sign of Suzanne, the boys, the bearers, the wolfhounds or the trunks. Bunny was in a frenzy of anxiety and began to receive condolences, like a bereaved widower.

There had been a series of dacoit* episodes on trains, with lurid tales of cut throats and slaughtered children. Wires were sent to every stationmaster along the line, but no one had seen the Morland family, until a few days later, when they all arrived totally unscathed. The story according to Suzanne was that there was this "delectable young officer" travelling down to Madras on the same train to join his regiment. "Bound to be killed, poor duckie. So why not give him a last happy fling?..." They had

---
* Bandits.

all got off at some nameless station and spent a couple of blissful days and nights, boys, bearers, wolfhounds, trunks and all...

That was Suzanne. She could have had any one of the husbands she wanted, including my father, but she never broke up a marriage. "Who wants those old fogies when there are all those splendid young chaps around?"

Suzanne had something called "panache". She would never behave like those wives in their limp cotton prints, who visited the men in the chummery* and left the car with the driver and the Union Jack outside, for all to see.

"That's just plain cheap," Suzanne said.

---

* Bachelor's quarters.

## *Chapter Eight*

By now, the heat was turned on like a tap, full blast, so Ooty-time was drawing near. The brainfever bird was screeching in the pipal tree, the woollen clothes were out of the storage cupboards and the house smelt of mothballs. At first I was apprehensive about returning to the brown hotel with all its associations of partings and death, but there had been an exciting new development and we were to share a house with the Dysons. Taddy and I were overjoyed, Jo less so, at the prospect of one more "little pest".

Our house was called Wildflower Hall and although it was certainly no hall in the baronial sense, nor was there any profusion of wild flowers, the two hot-weather seasons we spent there were bliss.

You drove the newly acquired Hillman up corkscrew bends to 7000 feet, while the rest of us chugged up on the train, with the engine pushing from behind.

Ootacamund (Ooty for short) was the Queen of southern hill-stations, a demiparadise of English gentility and nostalgia. Ooty reminded everybody of "home" but for me, who had never been "home", this was a new, shining, shimmering Ooty that was in no way associated any more with the colourless, shadowy summer of the year before.

Back to my first primeval memory, when you and I were one, Ooty was eucalyptus and wattle and mimosa. Ooty was heat and cold. Ooty was mist over the Blue Nilgiri mountains and woodsmoke rising from the valley below. Ooty was lying in bed at night listening to the thunderstorm clattering, pounding, raging on the rooftops, shattering the windows, tearing up the tiles, crying out its tropical, hounding vengeance, blowing out its fury, growling down the valley... rain singing softly, splashing, dripping... resting on the petals...

All this in a semi-dark room, with the fire still aglow and the nannies still mumbling... *This* was paradise.

Ooty was climbing trees. You never stopped me doing this and I spent hours scrambling higher and higher from branch to branch of the eucalyptus tree, to sit finally astride the highest bough, alone for hours, entranced by the view over the Nilgiris, the blue mountains that burst into one enormous carpet of blue flowers every seven years, with their long violet shadows in the brilliant morning light, turning purple against a charcoal sky when a storm was gathering. Ooty was the sudden freezing nightfall after the burning high-altitude sun of the day, darkness dropping like a blanket from the sky, with tiny holes for the stars to shine through.

Ooty was riding my first pony, the greatest excitement of all, in that first blissful, lightheaded summer, when everything seemed so right. Before, I had only ridden the stone statue of the sacred cow outside the Hindu temple in Madras.

My first pony was called Sandra and in the photograph I sit there like a queen surveying her subjects.

Mrs. Stapleton ran a riding stable somewhere down the hill, in a place full of trees and wind. She wore riding boots and britches all day long and she had a deep, barking voice, skin like shoe leather and a cigarette perpetually in the corner of her mouth. Her house was full of wet dogs and babies and she hung the babies' nappies to dry on the antlers of dead deer that were hanging on the wall or on the ears of the lion-skin in front of the fire. She was my hero and I wanted to be like Mrs. Stapleton when I grew up. When I told you this, you were horrified at my bad taste.

Riding became the passion of the next two years. I had "a good seat" but not enough "grip" so I was constantly falling off, but even when I was dragged two miles over the downs with my foot caught in the stirrup and my head banging all the way, I rode back home so as not to "lose my nerve" according to Mrs. Stapleton. That evening I collapsed with concussion and horrendous nightmares. "Could have broken her neck," Dr.

Willoughby Grant said, but I was riding again in a fortnight. "Real little trouper," Mrs. Stapleton proclaimed, but you looked decidedly pale and nervous as I went bucketing off again.

If I was not on a pony, I rode the garden fence or the back of the sofa. I turned my bed into a carriage, with two chairs for horses and a skipping-rope for reins and drove wildly over imaginary trails, until Jo said she couldn't stand it a moment longer. Jo and Taddy and I shared a bedroom, while Birdie and Hilda, the Dyson's nanny, slept in the day-nursery. Of course the sharing of Wildflower Hall with the Dysons is what made those summers so special. You and P.M. got on well and you soon turned what was, after all a rather dingy bungalow into a beautiful home, and the vegetable patch of a garden into a riot of bright colours.

Ooty is "a paradise for vegetables and flowers" people said and it is true that the vegetables in the bazaar were luscious and round and shiny, with the colours of precious stones, not the screwed-up, burnt-out stuff we got in Madras.

You never pretended to be English and you

retained your slight Greek accent and your foreign gestures and ways. But when it came to gardening, you "acted English" all the way, learning all the flowers' names and becoming a passionate gardener. But it was a genuine passion, acquired or not, and you had real "green fingers", bedding and coaxing and nurturing plants, as if they were babies. Even in this you were different. Your gardens were never like the English country gardens all over Ooty that reminded people of Sussex and Kent. They were somehow more unusual and imaginative with unconventional combinations of colours and flowers.

Sam came up with us and Cook too. How Father managed with Chokra in Madras, I don't know. There was a local sweeper with a lovely daughter and a baby with no pants on who lived in the garden and swept the paths with a twig broom (one of the early morning sounds of India) and emptied the thunderboxes when nobody was around.

Taddy and I were "best friends". With Jo it was not so easy, because Jo was never happy about anything. It was more than just the noise and mess we made; it was something deep inside that made her cross all the time. Perhaps it had something to do with her being P.M.'s stepdaughter, whilst Taddy was the genuine article. Once, when Jo said, "I'll tell Mummy," I said, "P.M. is not your real mother," and the hurt look on her face made me regret my thoughtlessness all my life.

Jo spent time talking to the grown-ups and learning things from them, while Taddy and I lived in a make-believe world all day long. "I never know who you are," you said, noticing our strange way of talking and behaving even at the dinner table.

Again, the house was full of friends. Old friends like Giles and Tony* and Lucas and George came up to cool off from the white-hot scorching plains, and Suzanne and the boys were somewhere around. But there were new friends too. Jerry and Rosemary Waterfield with their two little daughters, Hermione and Adrienne,

---

* Tony Mango joined Ralli Brothers in 1938. He was Managing Director of Rallis India from 1963-1974. He is Honorary Consul General of Greece in Bombay.

became special friends, as did beautiful, sad Pam Vincent with her three children, Charles, Detta and John. Their father had disappeared in the war.

Many people visited us at Wildflower Hall. You were as gifted at combining people as you were at combining flowers. There were the Averies, Dick, Linda and little Caroline. Linda had flaming red hair and a face that could have been beautiful if it were not so hard. She possessed something called "sex appeal" but she made everyone uncomfortable when she was around and she yelled at the servants and at Dick and Caroline too.

Dick was your friend. I knew this without really knowing. Your eyes lit up when he dropped by and his were dark and warm when he looked at you. Sometimes he held your arm lightly when you strolled in the garden. Dick made me happy for you.

With the troops coming up from the plains to convalesce, the house parties and dances began and the amateur theatricals too. The famous Welsh actor Hugh Griffith was there with the army and they put on *Arms and the Man* with

Hugh as the Chocolate Cream Soldier and our friend Jilly Cockburn as the leading lady. You designed the costumes and I saw so many rehearsals that I learnt the whole play by heart.

Then there was *Lovers' Leap*, when P.M. and Rosemary fell out over a white evening gown and you had to intercede. And a wonderful Victory Variety Show, with *everybody* performing, even the parson's wife, who danced the dying swan in a spangly net skirt, with the cardboard chandelier hanging upside down by mistake.

The heroic little Hillman chugged up and down the hill, to Saint Stephen's for memorial services, to Spensers and Higginbotham's for provisions and books, to the Ooty Club for curry lunch, to the downs and the lake for picnics, to friends for tea, to the "tat" races and the point to points. We were on the move most of the day, with long walks in the woods in the afternoons. But just before nightfall, a regular seven o'clock so close to the equator, the chopped wood was carried in and the fires lit in every room. This was the quiet, inward time before our supper, when I sat at your feet on the rug and watched the wooden bridges of firewood collapsing in the flames of imaginary burning cities, while you read your book or knitted, and I knew that nothing and nobody could ever break the bond of love that existed between us, and that all that happened during the day was never as important as that firelight time when you were there with me.

Taddy and I meant well, but we managed to be in big or small trouble most of the time. First we cut down a sapling in the wood with a kitchen knife and it came down on the roof and smashed half the shingles. Then a boy with freckles called Ken, who lived next door, found a small snake in the grass and we put it on a stick and carried it into the nursery to scare Birdie and Hilda and the snake was crawling up the stick towards Taddy's hand with its tongue flicking. Finally we threw it behind the house and it landed on the roof and when we told P.M. she said it was a krait and if it had bitten one of us, we would have been dead in five minutes. "And who says it won't come down the chimney?" Jo remarked.

But our worst escapade had to do with the

Maharajah of Jodhpur's wives. That was *big* trouble. Taddy and I spent many hours on the garage roof watching the cars go by, and day after day we watched this annoying little green car stuffed full of veiled ladies, driving past our garage, up to the Maharajah's palace at Aranmore. First we threw a couple of pebbles, but still it kept coming, then some handfuls of mud, to no avail. Finally we chucked a whole bucket of water over it and to our delight, there was no green car the next day. We watched the empty road from our rooftop and gloated on our success. But a couple of days later our luck ran out in a big way.

With a loud knock on the front door, there stood an immense turbaned man with a staff the height of a telegraph pole, demanding to speak to the Sahib. As bad luck would have it, Father was up from the plains and it was to him that the Maharajah's majordomo made his dire complaints about "the ladies being too afraid to drive to the palace, because the missies throw things at the car."

Father's explosion was of biblical proportions,

not so much because of our "filthy manners" but because he did business with the Maharajah of Jodhpur. We were made to write a letter of truly grovelling apology, full of "humble servants" and deliver it at the palace ourselves with Driver hovering in the background. The misery of it was that the green car was back the next day and we were never ever allowed on the garage roof again.

Our education was scrappy to say the least, which is, I suppose, why we were running so wild. Jo had lessons with P.M. and you tried to teach me Greek, without much success. Taddy and I had piano lessons, with Taddy playing Schumann's *Kinderszenen*, while I was still thumping out the scale of C. I could pick out almost any tune with my right hand, but the fingers of my left refused to obey and were always hitting the wrong keys.

Finally you took me to a dames school run by a kind old lady of "straitened circumstances" called Miss Barnaby who lived in a Tiggy-Winkle* cottage overlooking the downs. We read the

---
* re Beatrix Potter.

*Flower Fairies*\* and *Now We Are Six*\*\* and we painted pictures with watercolours. We learnt about butterflies and how bees make honey and we pressed flowers between tissue paper in big, heavy books. We did numbers on bead frames, pushing the coloured beads backwards and forwards, and we learnt how to make woolly balls for kittens to play with, out of cardboard and wool.

We sang and danced and planted seeds in the garden, and after a couple of hours we all went home, totally contented. I think this was the best school I ever went to and I will be grateful to little Miss Barnaby all my life for opening up a world of beautiful words and colours and sounds in such a happy, easy way.

So in spite of the Maharajah of Jodhpur's wives, that first Wildflower Hall summer passed as a lasting measure of happiness against which all subsequent summers could be contrasted and compared.

---

\* Cicely Mary Barker.
\*\* A. A. Milne.

There was a chill in the air, which meant winter was coming to the Nilgiris. The Dysons went down before us and the house seemed empty for a couple of days. Birdie asked, "Are you sad that your friends have gone?" I was not sad. I spent more time with you and we talked about ancient Greece and read *The Heroes\** and *New Tales from Troy\*\** and agreed that Achilles was a spoilsport, always sulking in his tent, whilst Hector was the true hero and the only one that Homer really loved. Now it was Troy burning when the logs collapsed in the fireplace.

One of the great things about you was that you respected my silences and did not ask, "What are you thinking?" as others did. And I respected yours. I could see that you were worried and distracted and Father never came up again after the Maharajah incident. We went for long walks together in the magical Ooty woodlands, full of fairy toadstools, the real red ones with white spots, and arum lilies a yard high and red hot

---

\* Charles Kingsley.
\*\* G.B. Harrison.

pokers and climbing vines and the trees hugging and kissing above our heads. We didn't talk much on these walks because we were both thinking, but there was no need for words. Once we got caught in the rain and I held your hand in my pocket all the way home to keep it from getting wet. There wasn't much I could do for you the way you did things for me, and I was not demonstrative with my feelings and often naughty and disobedient. Only little things, like keeping your hand dry in my pocket.

*Chapter Nine*

Back in the plains, Father said I had become a regular ragamuffin and it was high time I received some proper schooling. So it was back to Church Park and no nonsense this time. One of my most lasting early-morning memories of Madras is the children walking to school up Commander-in-Chief Road, the boys in their immaculate white shorts and shirts and the girls in their lovely salwar kameez,* all tinkling bangles and tinkling voices, with fresh flowers in their hair.

So now I was a real schoolgirl too, with a freshly washed and ironed frock every day and

---

\* Knee-length dress worn over narrow trousers.

matching hair-ribbons, but no flowers in my hair. I drove to school in the back of the Humber with Father, who dropped me off on his way to the office. I had a three-storey tiffin can with my lunch and a satchel for my books.

The first day of school I was nearly sick in the car because of the sinking feeling in my stomach and my heart flapping like a butterfly on a pin. Father in the front seat with his files was unaware of my panic, but Driver said, "Have a good day Little Missie... back very soon." That made me feel better.

Somehow I found my classroom, third grade, and wonder of wonders the whole room was scented with jasmine from the flowers in the hair of the little Indian girls. There was a nice plump teacher called Miss Rosalie welcoming each and every one of us at the door. The front row of desks was already occupied by the Government House and ICS children, the girls in cotton dresses, with their short hair parted at the side and held back with slides. The boys all seemed to have freckles on their noses to match their checked shirts.

I was put in the second row with the boxwallah children, mostly girls, with fancier dresses and longer hair, some with plaits and coloured ribbons like mine. Behind us came the lovely Indian girls all bangles and beads, which is where the jasmine scent was coming from, then a row of hot, plump Indian boys in their buttoned-up jackets (very high-caste, with a sprinkling of Maharajah's sons) and right at the back, the laughing, funny "bad boys" who were the best of all.

Miss Rosalie was Anglo-Indian, like Birdie, and very kind, but she was obviously terrified of Mother Mary-Teresa, whose habit luckily rustled along the corridor, providing the warning needed for us to stand up and say, "Good morning, Mother" in unison when she appeared at the classroom door.

Mother Mary-Teresa was so obviously not anybody's mother that it seemed a bit absurd to call her so, but I had decided not to get into trouble on my very first day. Also I sensed that poor Miss Rosalie somehow depended on our good behaviour. So it was up and down and

"Good morning, Mother" until the rustling receded and we could all relax.

Miss Rosalie was an excellent teacher and I soon discovered the wonder of learning. We could all read and write, so it was straight into arithmetic (the sixteen times table, because there were sixteen annas in the rupee) and fascinating Indian history (the laws of Asoka, the Dravidians, the Indo-Europeans, the Moguls, right up to Clive and the British). Geography was tracing maps on tissue paper, where the lines never quite met because the paper had slipped, but where we could colour in the mountains in brown and the plains in green and the rivers running all over the place in blue.

We learnt about the famous explorers, Columbus, Vasco da Gama, Bartholomew Diaz and Francis Drake, and best of all were the ancient sagas and stories from India, Greece and Rome. Biology was the breathing tube and the swallowing tube and our lungs like bellows puffing and our hearts like clocks ticking. I was in a constant state of amazement with this new world of knowledge that Miss Rosalie was unfolding before our eyes. In spite of the fact that the school was run by Irish Roman Catholic nuns, scripture was not compulsory and was taught in a separate room. With Christian, Hindu, Parsee and Muslim children, there were certainly enough gods and saints and prophets to go round. Personally, I preferred beautiful blue Krishna playing with the milkmaids to the rather insipid, sad-eyed Christian saints who were constantly getting their heads cut off or being stuck with arrows or eaten by lions, careless predicaments that Krishna would never tolerate. But I kept my preferences to myself, as nobody said we needed to choose, anyway.

Because of the multitude of religious holidays, there were always some children missing from the classroom, but that was no problem either. I managed my lessons quite well and Miss Rosalie seemed satisfied, until it came to sewing. That was a total catastrophe. Miss Rosalie distributed a piece of white cloth to each girl, with a needle and thread, and explained that we were to hem the cloth all around and then by sewing up the sides, produce a shoe-bag. With infinite patience, Miss

Rosalie went from girl to girl to show us how to do it. "Hold the cloth in your left hand, and the needle with your right. Turn down the edges and tack it all around. Then with small, neat stitches, with the cloth going from left to right, start to hem, moving your hand from right to left."

While the other girls were stitching away merrily, there was I with the cloth in my fist as the stitches grew bigger and bigger and more and more crooked and the cloth grubbier and grubbier. It was my left hand that could never take orders that was defying all my efforts and moving in the wrong direction. Miss Rosalie came around to inspect our work and I was seriously tempted to drop mine out of the window before she reached where I was sitting on the window seat. Finally she held it up, genuinely perplexed at the deterioration of a perfectly good piece of cloth and said that it was certainly the worst sample of sewing she had ever seen in her life.

The matter might have gone no further, but at that moment of course, who should appear at the door but Mother Mary-Teresa, who bore my miserable rag off, holding it in front of her large bosom, by its tail, like a dead rat, with the equivalent expression of disgust on her face. All the Government House and ICS girls smirked and giggled and held up their immaculate sewing for Mother Mary-Teresa to inspect, while the lucky boys who were doing carpentry at the back of the class with round Mr. Vikram, banging nails randomly into pieces of wood, laughed out loud. Only the little Indian girls were kind and one of them slipped her cool fingers into my clammy, hot palm.

Altogether it was the Indian children who became my friends. In the lunch break, we sat under the great banyan tree and shared what was in our tiffin cans. They offered me the best titbits and afterwards we would walk together hand in hand and talk. With them I discovered a quieter, gentler side to my nature that was not all about running and climbing and shouting. I stopped bringing my bicycle to school and brought my dolls instead. We plaited each other's hair with coloured wool and my best friend Radha brought me a bunch of jasmine, just like hers. Her hands were for caressing and not for pulling and pushing, and her voice was for singing and not for shouting, and her feet for dancing and not for kicking. She taught me her ancient songs and dances and told me stories of Krishna and I told her about Hector and the wooden horse and how the Greeks burnt the city of Troy. The Government House and ICS girls kept their distance, which was all right by me.

Taddy was there, but in a class for older and wiser children. Once I drifted into a divinity class by mistake, just as they had got Jesus up on the cross again. The Sister was telling how they gave Jesus vinegar to drink when He was so thirsty and how the Roman soldier pierced His side with a spear, and blood and water came out. I was relieved when Taddy came banging at the window and extricated me. "What are you doing in there? Don't you know that there isn't a God!" Taddy could be very emphatic, especially as her father, Scrubby, said there was no God and Taddy believed everything Scrubby said. So how could I, her best friend, go to divinity class and listen to all that nonsense! I never went again, but I kept the God and Jesus business to myself because I was not quite convinced that Scrubby was right.

At home, I resumed the obsessive riding of my bicycle around the house in the midday heat and miraculously did not die of sunstroke as everybody predicted. There were many friends around and Father celebrated his 42nd birthday with a garden party on the lawn. There were coloured light bulbs in all the trees and bushes.

You and he resumed your walks up and down the lawn in the cool of the day and there was an appearance of calm, but only on the surface. Something was definitely wrong. Father took to sleeping in his dressing-room and while he was bawling on the telephone in the early morning to all the upcountry stations telling them what to buy and sell, I would creep upstairs and into your bed under the white satin counterpane, because I felt you were lonely. One day there was a real row upstairs, worse than anything I had even heard Jo and Taddy get up too, and they were champion quarrellers.

Father yelled and shouted and you shouted back. I was in the garden, utterly amazed that grown-ups could behave in such a childish way. It went on for quite a while, with Father's voice settling down to a rumble and yours growing shriller and shriller. It did not upset me unduly; I was accustomed to rows in the servants' quarters and in the street, but this was a bit too close to home for comfort. Finally there was the usual familiar sequence of slamming doors, and Father came to the upstairs window and looked down at me as I stood in the middle of the lawn.

"You have to leave your mother alone!" he ordered, as if I was to blame. "Don't go upstairs at all."

It seemed one of his typically off-key reactions, as far as I was concerned. So I used my own judgement and went upstairs to your room. You were sitting at your dressing table, very still, with your back to the door. You said, "Come in, my love," so I knew I had done the right thing. I just put my arms around your neck and we held each other very tight. You were not crying, but you were very white. White with rage.

Years later, I learnt what had happened. A letter had arrived in the post, from the woman

Father had an affair with in 1941. This, he very conspicuously left on your desk. When you enquired about it, he admitted that he was in contact with her again (she had somehow managed to reach England) and that he was seriously considering marrying her. You asked, "But there's a war on. What is to happen to the child and me?"

And that's when Father answered, "I haven't really thought about that."

Of course you knew about the affair, but as the person in question had left Madras and there was so much else happening at the time, the whole matter had seemed out of sight, out of mind. It wasn't the affair itself. It was the incredible callousness of Father's remark, "I haven't really thought..." that caused the uproar. It's that besotted he was, because he was not naturally an irresponsible man.

I knew nothing about it at the time, and life seemed to return to normal, with both of you keeping up appearances so that not even your closest friends suspected that there might be something wrong. Only the servants in their uncanny way knew without a doubt. Any ripple or vibration could indicate the total disruption of their own eternally unstable existences, and depending as they did on Sahib and Memsahib being together and keeping the house running, their immediate vision extended no further than next payday. To ward off disaster, Sam touched his chalked brow and mumbled fervent prayers each time the light was turned on, Ayah grumbled less audibly, Chokra ventured no new ideas, Water-boy pumped feverishly, Cook prepared delectable trifles, Mali revived the withered petunias and even Birdie ironed and snipped and sewed without singing *Tipperary*. Everyone was being good until the storm could blow over and be forgotten.

I spent more time with you, rocking the long mirror and asking incessant questions, while you did your nails and hair.

"Do people live to a hundred?"

"Some people do."

"Will you?"

"Perhaps."

"How old are you now?"

"Thirty-three."
"Like Christ when he died?"
"That's right."
"But you will not die?"
"No, not yet."
"Never?"
"Not yet."
"Will you live to a hundred?"
"Perhaps."

I worked it out in my mind. 100 minus 33. Sixty-seven more years.

We went to the races with Giles and the Dysons and the Morlands and William Bell won again! I never got over the excitement of those flat races, the starting bell, the thudding hooves, the last lap, the finish.

You and Father entertained a lot and went out a lot. You were greatly sought-after for your charm and elegance and there were no more rows. Being of a decidedly pessimistic nature, you were not a person to entertain false hopes, but perhaps you truly believed that Father might reconsider, if life ever returned to a time with a past and a future again. Certainly nothing more was said for the time being and the unreality of wartime Madras, as if we were suspended in space, as if the real world was somewhere else, continued. Certainly friendships were formed in that timeless time that lasted a lifetime. This was our reality. We knew no other. This and the war.

You showed me on the map what was happening in Europe, and the Japanese war was constantly on our doorstep. As children, our wishes on the new moon and on wishbones were always, "Please let there be no more war." This was all we knew.

## Chapter Ten

A particularly vicious heat wave and perhaps the underlying tension in the house made us decide to return to Ooty earlier that year. Even the sight of the woollen garments airing on the veranda made me feel hot and Birdie moved my bed under the fan, whilst you took to wrapping yourself in a wet bed sheet in order to sleep at night. It was a good thing that Father had taken to sleeping in his dressing-room, as he might not have relished a soaking wet bed.

Whether there was an official end to the school year, I don't know. The classrooms were thinning out, as families left for the hills. We just went when we were ready, no questions asked. How the nuns survived in those thick woollen habits in such heat was beyond imagination. I tried to visualize Mother Mary-Teresa running around in a bathing suit, but it didn't quite fit, as I was not at all clear what happened underneath her habit, whether she had proper legs or just black shoes.

We spent most of the last days at the Gymkhana Club. There is a photograph of Jo, Taddy and me lined up, by the side of the pool, wearing sagging bathing suits that had lost their shapes and hung on us like wet rags. No question of new bathing suits in the middle of the war.

So it was back to Wildflower Hall with the Dysons, for what was to be our last summer together, although no one knew it at the time. We went in laps and instalments, the servants, the Hillman and the rest of us. Madras to Coinbatore, Coinbatore to Coonoor, Coonoor to Ooty, partly by train, partly by car. The stony tracks jolted us all the way and the altitude made us giddy, but the higher we drove, the more my mind was saying, "Yes, yes, yes" with the first cool breath of air, the first scent of eucalyptus and mimosa, the first wisp of wood-smoke, the first band of todas.* And suddenly we were there, past St. Stephen's Church, up the hill, round the bend, through the gate, up the crunchy, gravely drive, to the front door, where a smiling Sam and a couple of shadowy servants stood waiting to greet us with many salaams. We were home. An incredible assortment of bundles and trunks were carried into the house by the shadows, with Sam officiating over distribution and Birdie bustling around saying, "in here... in there... over here... up there... under there" until everything had found its familiar place.

You walked into the garden and looked out over the hills. I followed you, but stood at a distance behind you, respecting your need to be alone. I could feel that you were not really seeing the mountains, but rather something inside you. You had told me the story of Orpheus and Euridice and I wondered if you would dare to turn around. You did and smiled, but the spell was broken. I think you knew that it was the last summer and the end. The Dysons arrived a few

---
* Tribal people.

days later and it seemed as if life at Wildflower Hall would be a reflection of the halcyon days of the previous year. But things are never quite the same and my primitive fear that nothing ever lasts and continues was founded in that second year.

You and P.M. got the household into its stride. Sam took charge of "the front of the house" whilst keeping a watchful eye on the happenings "backstage". Tali, who had travelled up in style in the Hillman, staked a territorial claim to the hearthrug and installed her black kitten in the wood basket, where it was in constant peril of being crushed to death when the logs were brought in.

Other friends arrived, supplemented by our regulars, Lucas, George, Tony and our beloved Giles. Once Taddy and I hid Giles's army cap in a drawer to prevent him from leaving because we loved him so much. The result was total hysterics as Giles was convinced that he would be court-marshalled and shot for insubordination, and Jo's disdain for our "utter idiocy" knew no bounds.

There were new faces too, from the army

convalescents. Two new friends called Bill and Tom, one fat and one thin, like Laurel and Hardy, became regular callers. They were manic ballroom dancers and had a book with drawings of feet going in different directions. The foxtrot was all the rage, and Bill and Tom were champion foxtrotters and took to twirling P.M. and you around the sitting-room with the book in one hand, counting one, two, three, four...We tried it out in the nursery with Birdie and Hilda joining in, but Jo said we looked like "dancing bears" and the truth is that it was impossible not to step on each other's toes and crash into the bedsteads, as we walked backwards in a definitely ungliding fashion.

A new arrival was Body Macintyre. He was some kind of civilian, not army at all, and Taddy and I thought he was a big boobie. He was ramrod tall and solid, with a smooth face and smooth hair and no time for rowdy little girls at all. Strangely enough, some of the ladies (not you, who saw through him right away) described him as "delicious" and "delectable" and various other dishy things and it was "Body this" and "Body that" all day long. We tried to devise some plan to have him court-marshalled and shot, but as he was not army he hardly qualified for such a heroic fate. Finally he made a fool of himself forever at the "tat" races, and to this day I am convinced that it was all our doing.

The tat races were an Ooty fixture, a parody of the Madras flat races and part of the racing season, which included real point to points with the riders galloping all over the downs. In the tat races, the main contenders were little Indian boys on the ponies that pulled the luggage carts in the station and offered gentle rides to some of the less horsey children. The races were a hilarious affair, where the little boys were forbidden any form of whip for fear of thrashing their ponies to death, but compensated with yelling and screaming and wild flapping of arms and legs and garments.

Occasionally an Englishman on a regular horse would join the race, just for fun, and this is where Body met his due, for all his pomposity and lady-killing airs, when ten minutes after all the ponies had reached the finish, his horse bore him home, at a slow canter, the wrong way round the track, to our incredible joy and the amusement of all the spectators. So that was the end of "Body this" and "Body that" and Taddy and I never had a moment's doubt that wishes could come true.

The trouble with that summer was education. I no longer qualified for Miss Barnaby, and Father, who always interfered in the wrong places, said I couldn't run wild for six months and needed to continue my schooling. There was a regular British school in Ooty called St. Hilda's. We used to see the pupils walk by and sometimes tried to imitate their grey uniforms so people would take us for St. Hilda's girls. But that was as far as it went, and I never envisaged exchanging my tree-top existence for a new school. Rather reluctantly, I believe, you took me to meet the headmistress, who was appropriately called Miss Nettlebed. "Please don't laugh, darling," you pleaded. Faced with Miss Nettlebed's beady eyes, shelf-like bosom and large mustache, the last thing I felt like doing was to laugh, especially as this constituted my first encounter with those formidable, sexless creatures who insisted on teaching children and were to warp my concept of the difference between men and women for many years to come.

Even you wilted under Miss Nettlebed's penetrating eyes, and your slight foreign accent became more pronounced. In answer to her probing questions, you answered loyally that I was good at this and good at that, which in the relaxed atmosphere of Church Park was probably true. But before I knew what was happening, I was enrolled in a class where all the children were at least a head taller than me and endowed with a degree of Anglo-Saxon arrogance that completely obliterated my hitherto considerable self-confidence. There were no Indian children. They could not have survived in that suffocating atmosphere. Scared stiff and incapable of writing fast enough to copy what was on the blackboard before it was rubbed off, I dropped my pencils, spilled the ink well, felt my legs turning to lead and everything going blurred before my eyes. Finally I wet my pants, drip-drip down the back of the chair and the puddle on the floor, with all the children sniggering behind their hands, and then most terrifying of all, I couldn't breathe. The air just wouldn't go into my lungs and I was gasping like a beached carp. Miss Nettlebed sent me home.

You never made a fuss about cuts and bruises and minor ailments, but you always knew when something was really wrong. Doctor Willoughby Grant arrived with Miss Potts in his tiny Mini and diagnosed "nervous asthma" and saved my life. No more St. Hilda's. The air flowed back into my lungs and I climbed my tree to the highest branch and breathed again. Father was furious and said I was a sissy, but Willoughby Grant stuck up for me, and between you and P.M. we managed to have lessons where we learnt a hundred more interesting and important things than the silly calamity-tales that we had to copy off the blackboard at St. Hilda's.

There were periods of tension. Scrubby came up and yelled at our Sam for burning the toast, and that was the second time I saw you white with fury. There were also some minor dramas over the plays and shows that were produced that summer, but all in all everything seemed normal.

The war was still raging, but Stalingrad was delivered and the nine-hundred day siege of Leningrad had been raised. So that year's show was a Victory Show. The church choir sang: *There'll be blue-birds over the white cliffs of Dover, tomorrow when all the world is free* and *I'll see you again* and best of all: *Thanks for the memory*, where from the quiet, inward-looking expressions on people's faces I think that each person in the audience had their own special memory of some very special person. That's how memories work. They come back with a tune, with the words of a song.

The Victory Show had a beautiful final scene when everybody sang: *When the lights come on again all over the world* and one by one candles were lit on the stage. It was a sentimental time, but not soppy sentimental, because there were too many lists of those "killed in action" in the daily paper, and telegrams concerning sons and brothers and friends like Sid, who never came back. The sentimentality was just a form of hope. What was left in Pandora's box, you said, after all the furies were let loose.

We went for walks in the woods and called to

the echoing rock. We saw the gentians bloom on the Nilgiris, turning the mountains bluer than the sky. One night we saw a black panther scaling a tree in the moonlight and another night we were visited by a real live Princess, the Maharani of Baroda, who was like a golden idol shining and shimmering from the top of her auburn hair to her full length fox fur and the silver toenails of her feet. This was the wonder of India, not the disastrous, conventional self-righteousness of St. Hilda's, where everything smelt of disinfectant and turpentine.

But I caught a phobia that year, that was the other face of India too. It was impossible not to be aware of the ragged, human scarecrows that begged in the streets, twisted limbs dragging in the dust, fingerless stumps of arms thrust through the car window, cries of hunger and despair, the tap-tap of the blind man coming round the curb, the sores, the bloodstained rags, the filth, the flies, the horror.

In Madras, the beggars were more camouflaged by the general chaos of the bazaar but in Ooty they were everywhere, descending on us like a flock of famished vultures whenever we emerged from the car. It was impossible not to ask, "Why are they like that? What has happened to their arms, their legs, their eyes?" Over and again the standard answer was "leprosy". My secret fear was such that I became an expert on leprosy, collecting information from anybody who would volunteer often erroneous facts and details of this horrifying disease. The medieval belief that leprosy is transmitted through touch certainly persisted in the servants' quarters, and that is where most of my information came from.

One day we drove down to Spencers, just you and I, to pick up some provisions. "Stay in the car," you said, "I won't be a minute." Unfailingly disobedient, I followed after you and fell, literally, into the arms of a crutch-wielding, legless beggar, a bundle of filthy rags, who was passing on the pavement between the parked car and the entrance to Spencers. I can still feel the electric shock of terror, and my scream brought you and half the management and clients of Spencers rushing out. The beggar had moved on, as I crouched on the pavement screaming like a maniac, too terrified to even tell you what had happened. I never told you, but I was totally convinced that I had caught leprosy and was going to die. I regularly examined my toes and fingers and skin for the first telltale signs and although the normal rhythm of daily life diffused some of my panic, I lived with my poisonous secret fear for many years.

You were not well that summer. Your back was giving you trouble and you spent many hours lying down on the sofa in your room. Instinctively I tried to be less rowdy and noisy, and we spent time together reading and talking. You taught me so much, especially through your inimitable way of seeing things differently from what they outwardly seemed. Your sense of beauty, of wonder, of expectation. There were no closed doors. But you were sad. This you could not hide from me. Sometimes Dick came visiting. He would sit beside you and hold your hand and you would talk quietly and be together. When he left you would lie back on the pillows, with your eyes closed, very still, and once when I let him out the front door, I said,

"Please come back again soon, Dick." It came out without thinking and he looked at me with his grave, dark eyes and said, "I wish I could, little one. I wish I could." But he seldom came and I wondered yet again at the complexities of the grown-up world and decided never to grow up.

There were balls for the officers and dances for the other ranks. Birdie had a boyfriend called Ken. She never brought him to the house, but we had seen his photograph. One night, after the Dysons had left, Birdie had gone to another-ranks party and I was asleep in my room. Suddenly one of those crashing, banging tropical storms blew up and, thinking that there was no one else in the house, you came into my room in your see-through flimsy nightie to make sure that the windows were closed and no rain was coming in.

You found Birdie and Ken in bed together, the three of us all cozily in one room. I was fast asleep, but at your exclamation of "What's going on in here?" poor Ken leapt out of bed stark naked and Birdie dived under the sheets and I woke up to the extraordinary scene of you standing there in your see-through nightie confronting a naked, quaking Ken. What you said was, "I'm going to put on a dressing gown and I'll be right back." In his confusion poor Ken saluted out of habit and said, "Yes sir!" Then he scrambled into his pants and shirt and waited there, at attention, until you returned. I heard you say, "If you have got Birdie into trouble, I will be speaking to your commanding officer," and Ken was saying, "Yes Ma'am" and "No Ma'am" and something about... "walking Birdie home... and the storm blew up... and to get out of the rain..."

And there was I sitting bolt upright in bed, enjoying every moment of it. So you turned him out of doors in the rain and nothing more was ever said. I wasn't at all clear what kind of further trouble Ken could have got Birdie into. To me it seemed like a perfectly reasonable thing to do to get into bed with her to keep warm until his clothes had dried and the thunderstorm blew itself out. But I kept my ideas to myself and I know you never talked to his commanding officer. That's how fair you were, then and always.

## Chapter Eleven

The war was still very much in evidence. The Russian campaign was still raging, but the Allies had landed in Normandy and were liberating France, while another lot was moving up the boot of Italy. We saw the film called *Desert Victory* and we stood on our seats and cheered, although when I remarked that Rommel was much more handsome than Montgomery in those baggy shorts, Jo said, "How can you say such a stupid thing? Rommel is German."

At home P.M. made us each draw one of the scenes from the film. Taddy and Jo made wonderful pictures of all the soldiers fighting and winning, but all I could think of was the man with his mouth wide open yelling, "Fire!"

The Waterfields became our friends for life

and I have told Hermione many things she cannot quite remember about our time in Ooty together. Of course there had to be a memorable near accident, that summer too, when my bicycle brakes failed and I went careering down a hill to land plump in the middle of a Hindu wedding procession, where I was picked up and dusted off and cooed at by all the bejewelled, saried and scented ladies, *Missie Baba... Missie Baba...*, and borne back to the Waterfields' cottage, incredibly embarrassed, in somebody's arms in case I had hurt myself.

Father arrived for a short holiday and it was fun to have him around, until the "plans" began. One evening I was summoned to the drawing room and Father announced that the German occupation of Greece had ended and that you had decided to go home to see your parents, but that I could not go with you because the war was not over in Europe and there were epidemics and something called a "civil war" beginning in Greece. Also, he certainly would not look after a naughty person like me, so I was to go to a boarding school in Kodaikanal. I noticed that you said nothing at all and it all sounded so preposterous that all I said was, "I'm going with Mother." And Father said, "You can't." But by the way you left the room, I knew you would never go without me, so I didn't worry unduly, except for knowing in my heart that we would never ever be coming back to Ooty.

No more was said about the "plan" as something called the Battle of the Bulge was holding up the anticipated end to the war. Father went down to the plains and quite soon the Dysons left too, but we stayed on and on. I suppose with the trouble between you and Father, it was easier for you to be apart, but it started turning cold in Ooty and there was something sad about the Dyson-less house. I spent hours on the window seat looking out at the windblown garden, while Birdie brought out the thicker jumpers, all the servants shivered and Sam took to wearing his muffler pointedly around the house. You read a lot and the fires were lit as soon as the shadows grew longer in the afternoon.

There were people who stayed on in Ooty all the year round, mostly people of "straightened circumstances" like Miss Barnaby. There were teas and bridge games at the club and people spent more time in the Nilgiri Library borrowing books and reading the papers. You chatted to our kind neighbours, the Maconochies, over the fence and we visited an old lady who had danced with the Prince of Wales in 1922, long before I was born. Government House was boarded up and the Maharajah's palaces too, and all our army friends had returned to their regiments. Altogether there was a closing-in of time, a bleakness, that made the days too short and the nights too long, and a deadening kind of sameness that owed its origin to another place and another climate. "So like Suffolk," someone said.

At last the order came from Madras and we were on the move. The rhythm quickened and I was dispatched to the garden, so as not to be under everybody's feet. I climbed my tree for the last time and put some eucalyptus leaves in the pocket of my dungarees, for remembrance. I saw Dick walk slowly up the drive and instinctively I stayed where I was, so as to leave you alone together. I waited until he had walked back down again, with his head bowed, and only then did I come in. I found you in the drawing room by the fire, crying softly. There was nothing I could do, so I did nothing except love you in my way and respect your grief, your desperation, your need for silence. You were far, far away.

The Bay of Bengal monsoon had broken early that year and there had been terrible floods in South India. The river had overflowed and whole villages had been washed away and people drowned. There was a muddy high-water mark around our house and Mali had killed a king cobra in the garden. Mrs. Buck, whose house was in a hollow by the river, had been flooded out completely. A dead cow had floated in her back door, had circled her dining-room table and had departed majestically by the front entrance. Finally she took refuge in a tree for the night, waiting to be reached by boat the next morning. At first light she discovered that the tree was infested with snakes. "At least the snakes behaved like gentlemen and did not attack a lady," said the incomparable Marie Buck, "whilst the water-rats tried to bite my toes."

Actually the monsoon was an incredible experience, but I was glad to have missed it that year, with so much talk of snakes and rats. The sky would turn leaden and then pea-green-black in the middle of the day, and the water would come down in torrents as if the bottom of the sky had fallen out. We put buckets under the eaves of the house to collect rain-water to wash our hair. "Very shine," Ayah said. Better than the coconut oil they used.

While I was away, Father had cut out and pasted carefully in a drawing pad all the *Curly Wee* instalments from the Madras Mail. This was the kind of thoughtful gesture he would make to express his affection for me. I have them still. Count Curly Wee was a fixture of Madras life and a hero and paragon for us all. He was a very wise and noble pig, always fully in control of every situation. He had just climbed Mount Neverest with his dog companion, Ginger Dick. He had beaten the cheating Mr. Fox at the Great Bicycle Race, had cleared the name of Cuthbert Colt and had found the Missing Mouse, always retaining his composure and exquisite manners. The sketches by Roland Clibborn were enchanting, as were Maud Budden's rhyming couplets:

> *As Curly Wee sat reading in his library one day,*
> *"You're wanted on the telephone," his butler came to say,*
> *"I told them you were busy, but they wouldn't take a 'no' –*
> *"I couldn't catch the name, because the voice was queer and low."*

In Madras, life returned to a kind of arrested, suspended normality. I was back at Church Park but my world was not as secure any more. Grown-ups did and said childish things, they shouted and quarrelled and cried, and whereas ignorance made me feel vulnerable, knowledge gave me an edge on the fearfully vast extent of adult experience. So I tried to learn anything and everything I could, not only at school, but mostly from grown-up talk and servant talk. I acquired a ragbag of information which, lacking any measure of judgement, I stored randomly in the corners of my mind. I learnt to make associations out of knowledge and memories, I watched and took stock of what was unusual in people and situations, I collected words and tunes and images, while outwardly continuing to be my half-tamed self.

There was one more almighty row upstairs between you and Father that sent Mali diving into the flowerbed, as if lightning had struck him. I thought it might be the "plan" all over again, but I knew you would never leave without me, however much Father ranted and raged.

You both kept up appearances but there were stony-faced silences, with Father picking on me and yelling at Sam. Birdie confined me to the nursery "until the storm should blow over" and Driver took me to the Dysons or the Harocoposes most afternoons after school. Although Taddy and I talked a lot about a hundred different things, she never told me that her parents were fighting too, as I never told her about the shouting upstairs. Certain things just get worse if you put them into words.

Christmas came and went, with Father Christmas appearing round the bend of the Adyar River in a punt. Taddy and I and Basil still squatted on the lawn for the Punch and Judy

*Riding the holy cow.*

*Riding became
the passion
of the next two years*

*The Aetos in Madras harbour. You and Rosie and Tony Mango
with Commander Toumbas and officers.*

*Wildflower Hall, Ootacamund. 1943*

*Back to my first primeval memory when you and I were one.*

*Left: We went for long walks together in the magical Ooty woodlands. 1944*

*Right: You were wonderful with flowers.*

*The "tat" races were a fixture at Ooty. Body, you, P.M., Taddy, Lyki. 1944*

*Jo Dyson*

*Something was definitely wrong.
Madras, 1945*

*I rode that bicycle obsessively round and round the lawn.
Madras, 1945*

*Last birthday party at Delphi. January, 1945. (see page 177)*

*The Ghindy flat races, Madras. We went to the races with Giles and the Dysons, and William Bell won again*

*Lucas Ralli, the son of Father's big boss, with Tali and me on the lawn at Delphi*

*The last day but one. 14 April 1945*

*The sculptor Yiannis Pappas. Alexandria, 1945*

*A small girl with a sad expression.
Alexandria, 1945*

*Saturday's Child.
Athens, Greece*

show, but Jo sat with the nannies in a wicker chair and crossed her lovely legs, like a lady.

You organised a fancy-dress party for my eighth birthday. There we all are in a row. Jo and Taddy in authentic Breton costumes, Hermione as a pretty Russian girl and Adrienne as a fairy, Allister as a caveman, me as Colombine, a Dutch boy and girl, a ballerina, someone in a hula-hula skirt and an assortment of dressed-up babies crawling in the foreground. Only Charles Cockburn was too old to dress up like a sissy, so he stands there at the back, saluting like a soldier. There is an equivalent photograph of us all at the Ghindy races. Giles, so young and handsome, P.M. in a tiny "delicious" hat, you stunningly elegant all in white linen, Jo looking disdainful, Taddy looking eager, me all eyes. At least these long-ago, faraway pictures are unquestionable testimony to a group of people who spent the war years in Madras, India. No one can say it is all in my mind.

1945, and the countdown to our final departure from India had begun. How and why Father let us go is a question better left unanswered. The war was still not wound up in Europe and was raging in the Far East. Civil war had broken out in Greece and there was no air or sea transport between India and the rest of the world, except for military personnel. Even our passports were stamped "not valid for Greece". But you were determined to go home.

The last few months started out normally enough, as far as I was concerned, with no noticeable signs of impending change, except that you had started to collect trunkloads of clothes, sheets, blankets and bolts of cloth for the family in Greece. Every size of shoe was lined up on the porch and the new tailor ran up sundresses and shorts for all the cousins, while the Little Flower Orphanage produced exquisite party gowns and embroidered blouses for the aunts. All this was carefully wrapped in tissue paper and lovingly packed in great iron trunks to be shipped to Greece.

As a last-ditch effort, you tried to drum some more Greek into my head, while Father taught me a preposterous Greek poem about a black bird bearing the sad tidings from Constantinople to Greece, that the Patriarch had been hanged by the Turks. I understood very little, but memorised it conscientiously nonetheless, as Father assured me that these were the very first words I would have to recite to my grandparents when I arrived in Athens.

> *From the City comes a bird pursued*
> *Like a cloud on the north wind*
> *And clothed in black*
> *It cried and screamed:*
> *"Rise up, you fighting men!*
> *From East to West calamity*
> *The Patriarch is hanged!"*

Less prone to outrageous paradoxes, you started me on more basic concepts, such as the names of all my Greek relations, and making a sketch of Grandmother's house, you taught me the words for the different rooms. The articles were my greatest misery. How was I ever to tell if an armchair was masculine or feminine? More than my lack of proficiency in Greek, you were concerned about my English. From my association with Birdie and the servants, I had acquired the singsong intonation of Southern India and my English was decidedly Anglo-Indian.

"What will your grandfather say?" you asked. "Your Greek is so poor and you don't even speak the King's English." Not having had any association with the King, this was not surprising, but my grandfather's disapproval was becoming a problem.

Tali was returned to Mrs. Buck in a basket, where deeply affronted by such undignified treatment, she climbed a tree and refused to descend for three days. Subsequently she refuted domesticity altogether and reverted to a wild, jungle existence, where her cries in the night would waken the neighbourhood.

The sadness over our departure was all in the servants' quarters. No other memsahib was leaving for home from any of the other houses. Why was *our* Memsahib leaving and taking Missie too? Would Sahib need so many servants? Was it their fault? Had they done something wrong to make Memsahib leave? No one was talking or telling them anything, but of course they knew.

I acted as if nothing was happening, but somewhere in my heart there was an indefinable, deep, quiet sadness as I, with my eternal craving for permanency, found myself suddenly caught up in a transitory, totally unrehearsed situation.

Still, I carried on at school till the very last day. After the other children had left, I stayed behind to empty my desk, filling my satchel with all my copybooks. With so much coming and going of pupils, there were never any goodbyes, but still it was a strange feeling because this was not the hot weather where everybody left for the hills and drifted back in the autumn. This was forever. Also, I had no sense of "home" as being somewhere else. This had always been my home. Miss Rosalie, my teacher, came quietly into the classroom. All she said was, "You've been a good girl. Now you have to help your Mummy." It was a strange thing to say, but it made sense to me. At least she did not say, "How nice to be going home at last," which would have made no sense to me at all. But neither did she say, "You'll come back, after the war."

I suppose there must have been farewell parties and leave-takings, but I was not aware of them. On the evening before our departure, you called all the servants to the drawing room, not just the house servants, but Mali and Water-boy and the lowliest untouchable Sweeper too. As they lined up, you stood there and told them that you thanked them for their loyal service, that they should continue to serve Sahib and that you would never forget them. Then you gave each of them a small gift and a little baksheesh, and as you shook their hands one by one, they clasped your two hands in their palms and wept like small children. Sam placed a garland of marigolds round your neck and all they could say was, "Memsahib, Memsahib... no go our Memsahib..." and you cried too, and hugged them one by one, even Sweeper, who had never been touched by a white person or a caste Indian in her life.

I have no memory of the last night we spent at Delphi. It has gone. But on the last morning, the servants all lined up again under the porch and then, only then, did I hug Sam round his cummerbunded waist and burst into tears. I remembered how I had kicked him on the shin once, when I was very small, and I said, "I'm sorry that I kicked you, Sam," and he held me tight, so tight, and whispered, "Missie Baba, Missie Baba..." and I thought then and I know now that whoever has not gone away from Delphi, Commander-in-Chief Road, Madras, India, forever, has no right to talk of love.

## Chapter Twelve

In his diary, my grandfather records your last letter from Madras:

> I have hope again, after so many last-minute disappointments. I am determined to reach Greece and be with you. Perhaps the day *will* come. We try to follow the situation in Greece from the newspapers and the BBC and we are desperately worried. I wish you were all here with me in this peaceful land. Send me your news in any way you can. I need to know...

Then on April 3rd he writes:

> Wonderful news. Wire from Dora: *Leaving Madras for Jerusalem at the end of April.* Can it be true that I will hold her in my arms again? But she will find this country in ruins...

We left Madras on the 15th of April, 1945 and the long journey home had begun. Father accompanied us to the station and Driver carried our cases and bedding rolls and picnic hampers into the compartment. Birdie was travelling with us as far as Delhi. Father stood by the window as the train chugged off and there were tears in his eyes. You were quite calm, but you told me years later that you knew at that moment, without a doubt, that the three of us would never be together again, not in India, not anywhere.

The journey to Delhi was as episodic as all Indian journeys, although Father had arranged for us to be met by his company's upcountry people, with blocks of ice in gunny bags, at every station. The first evening, as I lay on the upper bunk, I saw the evening star, the most beautiful of all stars, shining in the sky, and a river of light seemed to be leading straight from the star to me.

Early next morning, Birdie joined us from her compartment to see that everything was all right and as the train travelled on through the vast hinterland of the Indian subcontinent, we watched the brown, burnt-out landscape slip past our window, mile after mile. At every station, the stationmaster would shoo the people off the roof, as well as the ones hanging from the windows, like crows, but as the train moved off, there they were all hanging on again. Sure enough, at the first upcountry station, a Ralli Brothers delegation was there to meet us, all salaams and smiles, as the coolies carried the ice blocks into our carriage.

But then a double minor disaster struck. A colony of ants invaded our picnic basket and infested the cold chicken, whilst water from the ice blocks managed to penetrate the wicker basket, so that everything was aswamp in highly contaminated upcountry water. There was no question of eating anything unless we all three wished to die dramatically of typhoid fever on the Madras – Delhi train.

At the next station, you went in search of a canteen, where you triumphantly discovered a dusty tin of bully beef. Appealing to the stationmaster for a tin opener, he informed you that as a devout Hindu, he could not open the tin nor permit his tin opener to be defiled. At the next station, a tin of pork sausages proved equally anathema to the Muslim stationmaster. Finally, somebody produced an omelette that made me so sick that I have never eaten an omelette again in my life.

However, by nightfall the miraculous Indian telegraph system had notified the next upcountry station of our predicament, and a delegation was there in strength again, with every form of provision for the final lap of our journey to Delhi, where we were met ceremoniously by the Ralli Brothers manager and his wife and housed in style in a grand mansion on Janpath Avenue.

Delhi was all marble porticoes covered in rhododendrons and huge wide boulevards running in all directions, with topied traffic policemen in boxes, waving their arms at every crossroad. You were wined and dined, while I rode a full-sized horse on the lawn with the syce* running beside me because my legs were too short for the stirrups.

---

* Groom.

Birdie washed and ironed everything we had worn on the train, and it seemed to me that this could constitute an acceptable end to our journey. All in all, I had no sense of distance or destination as far as our return to Greece was concerned. Each lap was a journey in itself and Delhi, grander and more glamorous than Madras but familiar in every Indian way, was good enough for me. I really had no concrete notion of where we were going but I trusted you implicitly to see us through.

The time came, too soon, for us to move on. Birdie repacked our bags and this time there were only two – a black suitcase and a green gripbag. Everything else was to be sent on, and the trunks with all the stuff for Greece had already been shipped from Madras. This was as far as Birdie came with us. Perhaps she left on the night train because I don't remember saying goodbye. She had a new position waiting for her in Madras, but she always said that I was "her girl".

Next morning I held Nippy, my black toy spaniel, in my arms because he had never flown before. How we managed to procure seats on that army Dakota that looked like a tin whistle, I don't know. Could it have been George of the Ritz working wonders again? Surely not.

Anyway, we flew off and bucketed about in the sky, in and out of the clouds, for a couple of hours and came down in Jodhpur where it was all of 110° in the shade. I was sick all over poor Nippy and then it was off again for some more bucketing until we bounced down in Karachi to be met again by the Ralli Brothers representatives, the wonderful Tombazi family. By this time I had had enough bucketing and bouncing and felt like a seasoned flyer with no need for any further "first experiences" especially as staying with the Tombazis was paradise on earth.

"Have we arrived? I like it here. Can we stay here forever?"

What impossible questions for you to answer. The Tombazis had two children, Alexander and Joanna, and a real Wendy Hut* in the garden, where we played all day long. I have no idea how

---

* re *Peter Pan*, by J. M. Barrie.

long we stayed, but all too soon the time came for us to leave again and this time, unbeknown to me, we were leaving India forever.

We boarded a new plane called an Ensign, beautiful as a silver bird, with a glass-fronted gallery up one side for walking and looking out, and a pantry for drinks and sandwiches. And who should be on the plane with us, but foxtrotting Bill and Tom, all dolled up in their uniforms, but still their usual smiling, joking, hugging selves! It made such a difference to be travelling with our two friends as we flew across Arabia in our silver bird, landing at an assortment of airstrips for re-fuelling, where it was invariably four o'clock and time for tea and the *pip pip pip Lilliburlero* of the BBC World Service.

We reached Basra after nightfall. The walls felt hot from the heat of the day, but there was a cool, night breeze from the desert as we ate our dinner on the hotel terrace, all together, by candlelight. You were smiling and laughing and it suddenly seemed as if everything was going to be all right.

Next morning, an order came that our plane

was to leave earlier than scheduled and there was a mad rush to the airstrip in an army jeep. We were bodily weighed in on the luggage scale along with our baggage and I was absurdly, and I presume mistakenly, hung with a label: "Not wanted on voyage".

Then off we galloped again, across the tarmac with fat Bill carrying me piggy back, Tom laden with our cases and you traipsing as usual in your high heels and narrow skirt. We only just made it up the gangway as the propellers were starting to whiz round. I think the change of schedule had something to do with picking up Sir Ronald Storrs* in Baghdad, as we had hardly been in the air for thirty minutes when we came down to a red carpet and a brass band and an honour guard of gloriously caparisoned, behorsed Bedouins and

---

* Sir Ronald Storrs (1881-1955), an Arabist, colonial administrator, and close associate and co-combatant of Lawrence of Arabia, served in Cairo, Baghdad and Damascus. He was appointed Governor of Jerusalem (1920-26), Governor of Cyprus (1926-32), and Governor of Rhodesia (1932-34). Ill health led to his retirement from government service, but not to the end of his involvement in Middle Eastern affairs.

up clamoured a red-faced, perspiring Sir Ronald, followed by two bearers carrying two enormous Ali Baba copper pots that were deposited in the aisle of the plane, blocking the entrance to the WC.

Worried by the unairworthiness of our beautiful Ensign, Sir Ronald kept banging on the pilot's partition, ordering him to go faster and faster. He also suggested that fat Bill should sit in the front seat to balance the plane. Noticing the only two female passengers aboard, he enquired about us and was told that we were a Greek lady travelling to Jerusalem with her daughter. The next thing we knew, someone passed you a copy of Thucydides' *The Peloponnesian War* with the compliments of Sir Ronald. A strange gesture of cultural complicity on this slightly insane expedition.

We arrived in Jerusalem in the early evening and parted from Bill and Tom and our last link with India. They escorted us, carrying our luggage as usual, to the waiting car of the Greek Consul and there were tears running down their faces as they hugged us and waved goodbye. Sir Ronald was ceremoniously borne away, copper pots and all, but not before you had thanked him for the Thucydides, which became a fixture of our onward journey. By this time, I was too tired and confused to take in much of what was happening, but out of the back window of the Consul's car, I swear that I saw Tom and Bill execute a couple of natty foxtrot steps, just for my benefit, before they disappeared from sight round the bend in the road.

They had been posted to Palestine, as far as I could gather from smatterings of conversation, because somebody called Mr. Balfour had made a declaration to the Jewish people at the end of the last war. There was so much that seemed nonsensical lately in the adult world that I did not even bother to enquire what Tom and Bill were expected to do about Mr. Balfour's declaration. We never saw them again.

The Greek Consul in Jerusalem was a kind man called Mr. Christodoulos, who took charge of us for what proved to be a much longer stay than we had anticipated. On that first drive towards Jerusalem in his grand car, with the

Greek flag flapping in the wind, you chatted quietly together, as I looked out of the window at the dry hills of Judea. Suddenly we crested the summit and there beneath us, her copper roofs glowing like amber in the setting sun, was Jerusalem. You asked the driver to stop the car and taking my hand, you walked with me to the edge of the crest.

"This is it, sweetheart," you said, "Jerusalem the golden. Remember, because it cannot come again."

I did not, for a moment, question your conviction that this was a totally finite moment, and I have remembered, Mother, all my life and blessed you for that moment of revelation that only you could have given me.

We stayed at the American Colony Hotel at the foot of the Mount of Olives, surely the most enchanting hotel in the world. So graceful, with its arches and balustraded verandas and its inner courtyards leafily shaded by orange and lemon trees. And a magical garden full of exotic trees and flowering shrubs.

In the open country outside Jerusalem, a

Turkish pasha had built a gracious residence for himself and his four wives. He died in 1895 without an heir. A group of Swedish-Americans rented and eventually bought the house. It became the American Colony Hotel.

Our room was spacious and airy with a door onto the veranda and wide windows over the scented garden. Obviously this was not to be a Basra-like stopover, because all our clothes came out of the black suitcase and the green canvas grip-bag to be pressed and hung in the cupboard. We wired Grandfather on April 27th: *Arrived Jerusalem on our way to Athens.*

He notes in his diary: "After six years of sufferings and hardships and disasters and despair, a ray of light and hope."

How to describe the two months we spent in Jerusalem, because this was the time it took for us to be issued with the necessary documents to continue our journey? The war was still unresolved in Europe and raging in the Far East, and travelling of "unauthorised persons" was forbidden. Perhaps the soothsayer was up to one of his tricks again. Having come so far, were we to stay here forever, or for what was still called "the duration"? You were tense and distracted and suddenly I became aware that for the first time in my life, home *was* somewhere else.

I was overwhelmed by a sense of estrangement, as if the basic concept of my own identity was unclear. I was angry with you for uprooting me and for transplanting me to this extraordinary no-man's-land where I was neither here nor there. Unsure of what was happening to me and deeply insecure, I questioned every rule and became undisciplined, disobedient and altogether impossible to manage. This was all you needed at this difficult transition in your own life, to have to cope with a hurt and unruly child. I forgot my manners and disgraced you in front of the Consul and your new-found friends in the American Colony. I broke the tender branches of the exquisite rare trees that the Italian manager had imported from all over the world to make the garden the paradise that it was. I tempted the other resident children into dangerous escapades. I disappeared and a search party was out all day looking for me. I got into a brawl with an enormous Arab who was beating his donkey senseless and was saved from certain death by the cook, who heard the screams from the kitchen. I pinched the Consul's little girl, who bawled all the way to the Dead Sea and back. In short, I was a social disaster. Particularly as your sense of what was seemly was not a question of conformity or self-righteousness but more a need for order, my disorderliness must have been extremely irksome.

With all the trouble I caused, I have sometimes wondered whether you regretted taking me with you. You could have gone alone and Father could have refused to let me accompany you on such a long, hazardous and unescorted journey, while there was still a war going on. He could have, but he didn't. So there we were together, for better or for worse, and there was no turning back. So much was certain.

You tried to establish a regular form of existence in order to counteract our displaced, limbo-like state. You even took to ironing our clothes with a huge coal iron, like Ayah's, in the hotel's washhouse. You, who had never ironed a handkerchief before in your life, were not going to allow our standards to drop because there was no Ayah or Birdie. Perhaps it was a form of occupational therapy, but the result was that, in spite of our meagre wardrobe, we emerged washed and ironed and beribboned every day.

The Greek Consul was kindness itself, as were all the British residents at the American Colony, mostly families of members of the British Mission who, with their headquarters in the beautiful King David Hotel, were trying to forestall the crisis that was looming in Palestine with the winding up of the British Mandate.

Slowly, very slowly, I began to settle down. Still somewhat suspended, but exhausted by my constantly embattled state and aware of your anxiety over a multitude of practical and personal problems, I buried some of my sorrow and gnawing nostalgia under an outward show of greater conformity.

## Chapter Thirteen

We settled into a daily schedule, as if we were to spend the rest of our life in the Holy City. India was always with me, but our final destination in Greece grew too remote to concern me any more, whereas for you, of course, this was the ultimate purpose of our journey.

Every morning we went to the Egyptian Consulate in an attempt to acquire the magic visas that would allow us to continue on our way. For some reason the walkway leading to the Consulate was strewn with arrested Egyptians, petty criminals who sat on the ground facing one another, so we had to step over their shackled legs. This you did daintily, whilst I enjoyed jumping over the aligned obstacles, as the cheerful thieves encouraged my efforts with laughs and applause. The angry argument between you and the Egyptian authorities that ensued in French invariably resulted in a stalemate, with the words "demain peut-être" putting a full-stop to the day's session, as the Consul meaningfully picked up his coffee cup and began to drink with loud slurps.

The Greek Consul, on the other hand, regularly escorted us to the Old City with his majordomo walking ahead, his symbolic staff of office of bound rods being most unsymbolically used to physically clear the way of beggars. We visited all the holy sites, the great Church of the Holy Sepulchre, the Wailing Wall, the Dome of the Rock, and at weekends we would be taken on drives to Bethlehem, Haifa, Nazareth and the Dead Sea.

One humiliating episode was when I found myself in a leaky boat in the Jordan River, being rebaptised for the third time, by a smelly old priest who was pouring muddy water over my head from a tin can and striking me in the face with a bunch of wet basil leaves. I was furious, especially as neither you nor the Consul or anybody else in our party was being rebaptised, and with my Indian background I was convinced that I would die of cholera if any of the holy water got in my mouth.

But slowly I began to absorb the wonder of Jerusalem and grow mesmerised by this extraordinary biblical city. In Jerusalem, Jesus was everywhere. I saw Him clearly, riding into Jerusalem through the Damascus Gate, on a small white ass. I saw Him leaning on a rock in the Garden of Gethsemane. I saw Him through a half-lighted window, at a long table with twelve bearded men. I saw Him turning to glance at Peter in the courtyard of the Pretorium, as the cock crowed. I watched Him stumbling and falling on the Via Dolarosa, bearing a great wooden cross. High on the hill, I saw Him hanging against the evening sky, as three women hurried by with bunches of myrrh and clean linen sheets. And most wondrous of all, I saw three men walking up a white, dusty road, until someone joined them and they were four. I saw Jesus everywhere in Jerusalem and this was my intense moment of spiritual awakening that was my secret, even from you.

In the early evenings, we would sometimes walk together, you and I, up the Mount of Olives, as far as the sad and magical Garden of Gethsemane, scented with mint and thyme, and then on to the British War Cemetery.* Too intelligent and unconventional to ever make a show of piety, you allowed me to jump from gravestone to gravestone. So many were inscribed:

*Known unto God.*

"What does it mean, Mother?"

"It means that Jesus knows who is buried here, even if we don't."

"And does he love them?"

"Most of all."

"And do they mind me jumping on their graves?"

"I think not. Perhaps they are pleased to know that someone is visiting them and that they have not been forgotten."

We visited a kibbutz, with children dancing and great fat cows munching in the barn. We

---

* Led by General Allenby, British forces supported the Arab Revolt against the Ottoman Empire during WW I. Jerusalem was captured on December 9, 1917.

wandered in the ancient city with the old Jews in hats and ringlets and the Arabs with songbirds outside every tiny shop. We ate strange bittersweet sweetmeats covered in honey and nuts... and time passed and passed in Jerusalem.

Greek Orthodox Easter came and the Consul took us to all the religious ceremonies. On Palm Sunday we joined the procession circling the Holy Sepulchre, with palm branches in our hands. Somehow you found yourself separated from me and further back in the procession, and frantic that I would be crushed to death by the pushing, shoving throng of ecstatic worshippers, you begged a huge, black Ethiopian priest who was walking just behind the Patriarch to extricate me. The priest picked me up in his arms and planted me firmly in front of the furious Patriarch, where I proceeded, palm branch and all, to lead the procession. What my grandfather would have called "my claim to sanctity".

Next day, we saw the Patriarch wash the other priests' dirty feet and then there was Easter with candles and fireworks and a great feast at the Consulate with red eggs and roast lamb.

"The servants don't get up when I go into the kitchen."

"Of course not."

"Sam always did."

"That was India."

"And are the people walking in the streets refugees?"

"No, they are just shopping."

I had never seen non-native people carrying shopping bags and walking in the street, except in newsreels of war refugees. It was clear that I would need to reinvent myself if I was to come to terms with this new world order.

Exciting things were happening. Just after Greek Easter, the war with Germany came to an end. Just like that. There was something called V.E. Day with bonfires and bells ringing, but it all felt a bit remote and it was hard to really celebrate when so many soldiers were dead and "known unto God" and others were still being killed in the Pacific.

Then the first ghastly photographs of the Nazi death camps appeared in *LIFE*, in a special edition that could be removed so that children would not see them. But I saw the pictures of skeletons in striped pyjamas either standing by the wire fences or lying in heaps, and I thought my heart would stop with horror. Disasters were crowding in. A boat had gone down in Greece with everybody drowned. At least two hundred people, the papers said, and many children. They were on their way to an island called Syros to spend the first free Easter after the German occupation. Tears ran down your face as you read the list of names. So many people you knew.

While the grown-up world seemed in total disarray, I was befriended by a lovely, gentle Romanian girl called Marie. She and her family lived in a small house in the grounds of the American Colony and I spent long hours with her. She was older than me, almost sixteen, and her life had been one long adventure, fleeing from the Nazis from country to country, until her family finally found haven in Jerusalem. She spent time with me and she sang me beautiful songs in all the different languages that she knew, lilting, soothing songs about love and loss.

Being with Marie made me feel quiet and safe and the jangling in my brain would fade away when she put her arms around me and somehow, across the years, I would like to thank you Marie, for being there when I needed you, my true friend, so much.

One day, two letters arrived from India. I watched you as you opened them and I saw that your hands were shaking. You sat down abruptly on the bed and your face went as white as a sheet as you read them, one by one, and then one by one again. I had no idea what was in the letters, except that I recognised my father's handwriting on one of the envelopes. After what seemed like a very long time, you said, "Please stay here. I just need to be alone for awhile," and as if you were walking in your sleep, you left the room without even closing the door behind you.

I was stunned most of all by my total exclusion. Even at the time of the great rows between you and Father in Madras, I had been included. Now you preferred to be alone. Typically disobedient, I waited a few minutes and then went in search of you. I found you with your friend, kind, round, powdered Mrs. Walsh, in the upstairs drawing room. You flew at me in a fury, saying something about my dishevelled, untidy appearance, which I knew had nothing to do with the true cause of your distress. The letters were still in your hand and Mrs. Walsh had her arms around you and signalled to me to disappear. I retreated back to our room. After a while you returned, not angry with me any more, but your face was bleak and drawn.

It took some time for you to compose yourself enough to propose a walk on the Mount of Olives. I would have understood if you had sent me to be with Marie while you stayed with Mrs. Walsh, but now I felt that in your silent grief you needed me to be with you. We didn't talk at all on that walk, we were both so full of thoughts, but for the first time in my life, I realised how vulnerable you were and that I could only help you by being there with you, inseparably bonded as we were to one another, for better or for worse. And so that there would never be tears in your eyes ever again, I would have given you the moon and the stars like in the fairy tales, if they were mine to give, but all I could do was to stand dumbly by and let you carry the burden of your grief alone.

Was our bonding founded on similarity? Did our natures coincide? Not at all. We could not have been more dissimilar. Our bonding was totally founded on unconditional love. Perhaps another child could have made you happier by answering more directly to your needs, especially as your outward ease concealed a nervous, susceptible, dramatic nature, and my elusiveness and tendency to drift out of reach when life grew too complicated filled you, who lived and breathed through me, with terror for my well-being.

I know now what was in those two letters that ripped your world apart and shattered the fragile store of hope in your heart. One was from my father and one was from Dick. I also know that *that* was the moment when what you would later call "the black bird" settled on your heart, so that even though you outwardly remained your charming, witty self, you never totally trusted anybody else again. You always expected desertion and betrayal and your obsessive, possessive love for me, so tempered by fear, became a burden that I was to carry all my life.

## Chapter Fourteen

After a long period, where it felt as if time had stopped in Jerusalem, we suddenly received our visas from the Egyptian Consulate and we were on the move again. Colonel and Mrs. Walsh* threw a farewell party for us on the last evening and even the Italian manager looked sad and forgave me for breaking the tender limbs of his rare trees. Marie my friend, lovely, gentle Marie stood by the gate and waved until we rounded the bend and I felt sick in my stomach and sad in my heart at having to say goodbye and leave again, when other people seemed to stay where they were. The Consul's driver drove us to the Dead Sea, which seemed an absurd place

---

\* Colonel Walsh was a member of the British Mission in Jerusalem. He was killed when the King David Hotel was blown up a year later.

to leave from, and there rocking slightly in the middle of the lake was a tiny sea-plane, looking more like a boat than a plane.

"Are we going to sail to Egypt?"

"No, my love, we will fly out of the lake like a seabird."

You and I, and the black suitcase and green canvas grip-bag, were loaded onto a motorboat and carried over the Dead Sea towards what looked more like a dead duck than a seabird. Dressed in your blue and white travelling outfit, elegant at all costs and in all circumstances, you had also acquired a beautiful white Ascot hat with an enormous floppy brim.

As we were being pushed and shoved off the motorboat and pulled through the sea-plane's door, a sudden gust of wind swept the hat off your head and into the Dead Sea. There was nothing to be done, except fish it out with a bargepole and hang it on the doorknob of the plane's WC, where it dried stiff from the salt in a decidedly unhatlike shape. You took it well and we settled on a bench, surrounded by a miserable assortment of exhausted army wives and pale, washed-out children who eyed us silently from under their crooked fringes. With a lot of whirling of propellers and splashing of wings, the seaplane rose vertically into the sky and started to weave and bounce about, until we were all sick and I prayed that it would crash back into the Dead Sea, so we could all drown and stop being so sick. Finally, after what seemed like a horrible lifetime, we plopped down in the Nile like a dead fish.

We stayed in style at the Shepheard Hotel, all gilt and marble and chandeliers and flies. An army of liveried servants opened car doors, carried cases, operated lifts, opened more doors, plonked down cases, swotted flies and waited expectantly for baksheesh. Everything was enormous, the doors, the beds, the cupboards, the bathtubs. I felt I had to shout to you across the room to be heard and I was overwhelmed by so much grandness. Immediately you busied yourself with our wardrobe. You rang for the maid to press our dresses and for the valet to shine our shoes, and when you laid out your monogrammed silver brushes on the dressing table, I knew that this was going to be another long stay.

Cairo in 1945 was the craziest place in the world. Nothing made any sense to me at all and I felt as if I was rattling around inside a huge balloon that was about to burst. The whole of Greece seemed to be in Cairo, the Greeks of Egypt and the Greeks of Greece, the Greek army and the Greek navy, the Greek Government-in-Exile and members of the Greek Royal Family.* They were all in the Shepheard Hotel and they all knew you and nobody knew me. If they had left me alone, I would have been perfectly happy, because the hotel was a paradise for exploring, but they all wanted to pat me and kiss me and pinch my cheeks and tweak my hair and talk, talk, talk to me in Greek. And even the talk would not have been so bad if it were not for the incessant, repetitive questions.

The ladies in hats and veils and swishing dresses and the men in uniforms and clanking

---

* After the fall of mainland Greece to the Germans in April 1941 and the subsequent fall of Crete, many Greek families fled to Egypt. A Greek Government-in-Exile was set up in Cairo, and contingents of the Greek army and navy joined the British army.

boots, in the lifts, in the hallway, in the dining-room, on the verandas, all asking me insipid questions and interfering with my life.

"What is your name?"

"How old are you?"

"Where did you live in India?"

"Do you like Cairo?"

And then the introductions and admonitions from you:

"That is the general." (Don't scowl, darling.)

"That is the Prime Minister's wife." (Please smile.)

"That is Mrs. So and So." (Say good morning.)

"That is my old school friend." (Let her kiss you.)

"That is your grandfather's colleague." (*Please* be polite.)

Why on earth hadn't they all stayed in Greece? Why couldn't they leave me alone!

On the second day the invitations began and we were swept up into a social whirlwind. Mansions like vast tombs with drawn curtains and rooms so dark it was impossible to see from one end to the other, and armchairs so enormous that the person inside was buried up to the neck. Dining tables weighed down with crystal and silver like Ali Baba's cave, with a confusion of five different knives and five different forks by each plate, and icebergs of grapes and exotic fruit that nobody touched and chandeliers with a thousand light bulbs in the middle of the day and huge urns with dead-looking greenery that should have been out in the sunlight and two life-sized statues of Nubian slaves on either side of the stairway that gave me the fright of my life. The only fun was sliding on the parquet floors that shone like deep-sea water, but this was definitely not approved of, nor was sliding down the banisters, or playing hopscotch on the black and white floor-tiles in the hall.

The houses of the rich Greeks of Cairo were overflowing with possibilities for games and escapades, but nothing like that was permitted at all. And I was bored, bored and fed up with all the exclusive grown-up talk, a new experience because in India grown-ups never talked over our heads as if we couldn't or shouldn't understand. Also, as if battling with Greek was not bad enough, all the Greeks preferred to converse in French!

At the Sporting Club one afternoon, a lady like a pillar of stone, with an enormous hat and a parasol like a pagoda, accosted me as I was running for cover and started asking me questions in French. I burst into tears. I, who never cried, started blubbering like a baby. It was just too much to bear. After that, people left me alone. "An extraordinary child," they said.

There were no children in Cairo. They had all left for Alexandria because it was already sweltering hot and soon most of the ladies began to leave too, which was just as well, as your men friends were much more relaxed and jolly.

One afternoon one of your generals, with a bevy of adjutants, took us to the Mena House Hotel for tea and then in an army jeep into the desert to the Great Pyramid at Giza and the Sphinx. There were a couple of Bedouins with camels and ponies and you allowed me to ride a pony all around the pyramid. That was my best day in Cairo, as the red sun dived behind the great man-made mountain of stone.

The heat was terrible and the flies could drive you insane. Someone bought me a fly swish with a horse's mane, dyed pink, but when I started swishing everything and everybody in sight, you took it away from me. At least the generals and the admirals and the ministers were not as snooty as the society ladies, and one big, fat admiral would stand at the foot of the great Shepheard Hotel staircase with his back turned and let me jump on his back from the fourth step. One day King Farouk came to the hotel. "Look Mother, Ali Baba! It really is him!"

But even this could not relieve my sense of alienation. Once again I had been uprooted and my life was on hold. Also, there was something about Cairo that gave me a feeling of revulsion and revived my morbid fear of disease. The twisted, inhuman forms begging outside the hotel, stretching out their withered arms in supplication. I avoided even their shadows for fear of contagion.

At night, after you went down to dinner, I could not sleep because of the heat and the ugly noise from the street below. The never-ending screeching of horns, slashing of whips, crying of wares, every sound jarring, dissonant, cruel.

Night after night, with my nerves on edge, every muscle taut and my head throbbing, I would ring one of the bells by my bed (the one with the picture of a valet) and the kind Egyptian valet would answer my call, all dolled up in his green uniform, and he would sit on my bed and hold my hand and stroke my hair with his long, thin fingers, making little, soothing sounds in his own language. Night after night, he stayed by me until my limbs relaxed and my brain stopped buzzing and I could sleep. He would leave as noiselessly as he came. I never told him why I rang, but he understood my need for company and would sit by me, with the wonderful silence and patience of Eastern people.

Somehow you learnt of these night visits and were horrified. You thought he might do me some harm. I had no idea why you should think such a thing, but next night when I rang nobody came, and I lay awake for hours in a state of misery which was almost like physical pain, until the roar of traffic lulled me into an unquiet, twitching, nightmare-ridden sleep.

## Chapter Fifteen

We left for Alexandria by train. I had stopped even asking where we were going. It made no difference any more. We were not really going anywhere in particular, just moving from place to place, constantly unsettled and unassimilated.

The back of my knees stuck to the seat and you tied my plaits on top of my head to cool my neck. The heat came through the window in red-hot blasts and became trapped in the compartment. I tried to read, but my fingers stuck to the pages. Finally I put Nippy in the window and we looked out together at the landscape of dry mud and dusty date palms and shrubs under a yellow burnt-out sky, while you closed your eyes and dozed and the train chugged drearily on.

*Where am I going, I don't quite know...* The line from A. A. Milne drummed in my head. Grandfather wrote in his diary:

Such joy! Telegram from Alexandria that they have arrived and await the earliest passage home.

Something inside me said "yes" when we arrived in Alexandria. Perhaps it was her beautiful-sounding name. Alexandria, city of Alexander. City on the sea, looking out across the wide stretch of water to Europe, to Greece. I felt I could breathe again, after the suffocating closeness of Cairo.

The sea breeze was fresh and salty. We stayed at the Hotel Metropole, which was less grand but more friendly than the Shepheard, and miracle of miracles, the four great iron trunks had arrived from India, unscathed after their long sea voyage. Even my bicycle in its wooden casing was there.

Once the trunks were opened and aired, you checked their contents for sea water, dampness and moths, and put them out to sun on the veranda, where they acquired the salt scent of

Alexandria. The arrival of our trunks meant a certain renewal of our wardrobes and in your immaculate linen suits you certainly rivalled any of the Alexandrian ladies for elegance.

There seemed to be many more real friends in Alexandria, not the migratory crowd of Greeks in Cairo, but families who had been there for generations. Again we were invited everywhere, but you were more in your element, the atmosphere was relaxed and there were children for me to play with. The Greek children spoke French, but no English, so I was compelled to communicate in Greek, even to the extent of translating the whole of *Curly Wee*, word by word, for my new friend Costi Stassinopoulos. There were the two Tsiganti boys, Lephteris and Memas, and Leon and Maria Carapanayiotis. Memas was older, with his own group of friends, but the other three, with little Costi tagging on, accepted me in spite of my foreignness, and we had a great time together. In the mornings we went swimming at the aristocratic beach of St. Stephano, with the striped bathing huts and the pier with its steel girders, like a walkway into the sea.

The parents sunned themselves in deck chairs, whilst the small children played in the sand, under the watchful eye of smart nannies in upright seats. It felt like Madras. Leon, Lephteris, Maria and I swam in the sea, a dangerous sea with strong currents and sudden north winds that made the waves billow high. The moment the red warning flags appeared, the parents and nannies ran to get the children out of the water.

The very first day I went swimming there, I nearly drowned.

"Can you swim?" Leon asked.

"Of course I can."

"Can you swim as far as the buoy? We call it Japan."

"Of course I can."

I was not going to admit that I could barely swim the width of the Gymkhana Club swimming pool. Halfway to the buoy, with the current tugging at my lead-weighted legs, I began to sink. In their panic and in an attempt to hold me up, the boys began to go under too, as the waves came over our heads. Bobbing frantically, drinking gallons of sea water, we were finally rescued by the ever-diligent life guards and towed ignominiously out to shore, to lie exhausted, coughing and spluttering in the sand. You were not there that day, a new round of negotiations with the authorities had begun, but the other parents were doubly shocked by the possibility of "somebody else's child" being drowned whilst in their charge.

"Why did you say you could swim that far?" the boys asked, too weak to even be angry.

"But I can, I can!" Even then my pride would not allow me to admit defeat.

In the cool of the evening, we went for drives in horse-drawn buggies, along the beautiful corniche, to see the sun sink into the sea. One morning you took me to visit a sculptor in his studio and that's when my new trials and tribulations began. Yiannis Pappas* took a fancy to my face (why I don't know) and asked you (not me) if he could make a model of my head. Something called a "bust" which is what I thought Miss Hardy had sticking out in front. So for two

---

* Famous Greek sculptor who died in 2005.

whole weeks, there we went every morning and while you drank lemonade and chatted with the lady of the house on the veranda, I was perched on a high stool as Yiannis transformed a lump of red clay into the shape of my head. Fascinated at first, I watched the deft movements of his fingers as he squeezed and moulded the clay, but by the end of the first week, I began fidgeting.

"Please sit still," he begged. "It's nearly done."

But next morning there I was on the stool again, because something was not quite right "around the eyes".

Desperate at last, he gave me *Oliver Twist* to read to keep me quiet. With full credit to the sculptor, not to me, the result is a beautiful work of art, a small girl with heavy plaits, head bowed and a sad expression round the mouth (for the sufferings of Oliver). Later, after we left, Yiannis carved the head in stone and showed it at one of his exhibitions. It was bought by a friend of yours and sent to us in London. I have it still.

Life could have been quite idyllic in Alexandria if it were not for your sadness. More letters had arrived from Madras and some from Greece, and the anxious pucker had settled permanently between your eyebrows, and the grooves had deepened around your mouth. The expression of your face was drawn and your gaze often so remote. Drifting far away, even from me.

"Why are you so sad, Mother?" I asked one day.

"What makes you think that?"

"Because you are. Sad and far away."

"It's nothing." You made an attempt to sound casual. "I'm still tired from the journey. Don't worry about me."

But I knew it was not the fatigue from the journey. Something was wrong deep in your heart, like a wound.

"Some people go through periods of sadness," you volunteered, "and then it passes."

But I knew that this sadness had a deeper cause and I could not bear to see you that way and to feel so helpless.

One day the boys said something about money.

"Your grandfather has lost all his money."

I asked you and you said, "Yes, it's true."

"But how could he lose it?" It seemed such a careless thing to do.

"Many people were ruined in the war. It was all in government bonds, mine too. All the money we had is worthless now."

I was not convinced that this was the only cause of your sadness, but I kept my thoughts to myself. You had enough to contend with. At times, I longed so much for India that it was like pain. I longed for the colours, the sounds, the heat, the dust and most of all for the lashing, pounding, tropical storms of Ootacamund. The rain like stones, pelting the tin roof and the window panes, and the wind like a dark torrent thrashing the trees to madness, the dampness in the sheets, and the wet bracken in the woods next day. *Drip, drip.*

I thought, "I will soon be nine years old. Perhaps at nine I might be afraid of the storms or, even worse, I might not care any more."

"We have to go back, Mother."

"Go back where?"

"To India. Before I'm nine. After that there won't be any point in going back. I will be too old."

"Too old!"

"The storms won't mean anything any more."

You must have had a brief vision of a repetition of our interminable journey in reverse. All you said was, "We'll go back, darling... perhaps not right away. But we will, I promise you. And you'll see that nine is not so old."

Again I was not convinced, so you added, "All I want is for you to be happy, darling. Please try to be happy."

"Why are *you* not happy, Mother?"

Time began to pass purposelessly in Alexandria. Grandfather wired: *Longing to see you both very soon.* But there were no boats to carry us home.

The war was still raging in the East and in shattered, bleeding and impoverished Europe, there were no victors and no vanquished. There was no post-war euphoria, but in Alexandria everything and anything, regardless of its seriousness, could be transformed into small-talk and gossip, and I think that with your infallible sense of pertinence and priority, this was beginning to get on your nerves.

You listened to the BBC World Service religiously, and wires and letters arrived from

Athens, but we were no nearer home and Alexandria seemed to be settling into a leisurely pre-war situation, as if there had been no war at all. We were kindly received, but as transitory birds of passage, we did not really belong and were easily overlooked by the permanent residents of this unreal city. We were unquiet spirits in a secure and settled world. Even the army people so distinct in Cairo were comfortably absorbed into the teas and soirees of Alexandria and became part of the social scene.

Only you longed to move on and reach home. We spent time in the British Consulate having our passports processed and stamped for Greece. But there was still no passage to Greece, only a rumour of a Swedish passenger ship, but nothing definite at all. Time grew heavy in Alexandria. We walked on the corniche and watched out for ships, as we kept more and more to ourselves. Why get involved in a world that was not our own?

You and I, in limbo in Alexandria, between two worlds.

## *Chapter Sixteen*

Then, as usual, everything happened at once. General Tsigantis arrived from Cairo like a hurricane, bursting with plans and ideas for our immediate evacuation. Why wait for the Swedish ghost ship when a contingent of the Greek army under his command was leaving for Piraeus on a British battlecruiser, incongruously named *Princess Catherine*? He would stow us away as his sister and niece! By nature, you were a law-abiding person, but considering that our whole wartime journey from India had been nothing but risk and adventure, General Tsigantis' escapade appeared no more extreme than anything that had gone before. Still you hesitated.

"What if we are arrested by the Egyptian authorities?"

"Trust in me!" was the General's imperious reply.

"How will you explain the presence of a small child on a battlecruiser?"

"Trust in me!"

"We have British passports and no permit of entry to Greece."

"Trust in me!"

Throughout his career General Tsigantis was either decorated for acts of bravery bordering on insanity, or court-martialled and condemned to death or life imprisonment as a mutineer. He had served in the French Foreign Legion and fought against the Italians in Ethiopia. For him there was no middle way and "operation stowaway" had certainly fired his imagination. Finally, your yearning for home overrode your misgivings.

On July 15th, 1945, three months to the day since we left Madras, you wired a delighted Grandfather: *The great day has come. Arriving Saturday.*

In utmost secrecy and without notifying any

of our Alexandrian friends, who could not have kept a secret in a thousand years, we slunk out of the Metropole late one evening. A car provided by your Cephalonian friend Panagis Yiannoulatos took us to the port, and there on the dock, ready to be loaded, were our four iron trunks and my encased bicycle. At the top of the gangplank, with a fistful of documents in your hands, we were accosted by the Egyptian harbour authorities.

"Yellow paper!"

Shuffling through the deck of papers in your hand, you could find no yellow paper.

"No board without yellow quarantine paper!"

The ship's funnels were belching steam and smoke and the engines were running, but again the General came to our rescue. An army jeep and driver appeared from nowhere and we were whisked off to the other end of the enormous harbour to a dingy shack, where a sleepy medical orderly announced, "Seven o'clock. No do. Tomorrow Friday, Holy Day, no do. Saturday do."

Frantically, you did something you had never done before. You plonked a wad of dinars on his desk. Without blinking an eye and only using one hand from the wrist down, an unmistakable gesture of nonchalant officialdom that I had come to recognise, he produced two yellow tissue papers covered in Arabic squiggles. Then, after a leisurely search for his seal and inkpad at the bottom of a drawer, he proceeded to stamp the tissue papers over and over again. Finally, pushing them towards us with one finger he said, "Ten dinars more."

Bundled into the jeep we hurtled back to the ship, just as the gangplank was being raised. Down it came again and up we rushed, as the ship came unstuck from the dock. But there, dejectedly, still on the dock, sat our four iron trunks and my bicycle! They could not be loaded on the battlecruiser, the General explained, but Panagis Yiannoulatos had promised to post a guard to keep watch all night and to store them safely in one of his warehouses next morning.

"And...?"

"And send them on, whenever there is a boat."

"And so we arrive in Greece empty-handed, after six years!" you announced dramatically as we watched our trunks receding and fading from view. "We will never see them again." To me it seemed like a minor issue, considering that we had nearly missed the boat altogether, but you were visibly upset.

The captain was most gallant and settled us in one of the officer's cabins, below deck, but as I felt sick the minute the ship set sail, he accommodated me in a camp bed outside his own cabin, on the upper deck, with a sailor to guard me day and night.

As the ship glided through the bay, the soldiers and sailors gathered by the railings to see the lights of Alexandria for the last time. In total silence, they stood and watched as the sun set and the city became a line of flickering lights which slowly sank beneath the horizon, leaving a reflected glimmer in the sky. And long after darkness fell and the city had disappeared too, they still stood there silently watching. And we stood there too, you and I, hand in hand, on the last lap of our long journey home, unknowingly bidding farewell to Alexandria and the East.

"And bid farewell to Alexandria, leaving you

now." You murmured the great Alexandrian poet's* lines. "As the God forsakes Anthony..."

Who was forsaking who? I wondered.

The sea voyage was an exciting new experience. I was adopted by the home-going troops as a kind of mascot. Memas, the handsome Memas, who had no time for little girls, and his brother Lephteris were on board with their father, the General's brother, and on the first evening we sat by the prow in the dark with the soldiers and sailors and, as the old battleship pitched and creaked they took up one of the ancient sea-shanties:

> *Sea with your salty water,*
> *Save the seafaring men,*
> *And bring back my love to me.*

I was mesmerised by the song and I truly think that this was the moment when I first realised what it is to be Greek. Little wandering waif, neither English nor Indian, displaced in a no-man's land of conflicting recollections, perhaps, perhaps I could be Greek.

---

* Constantine Cavafy (1863-1933).

*Don't you know, deep sea,*
*That the girl is too young*
*And black does not suit her?*

I thought of Marie and her beautiful songs so full of longing, and I think I fell asleep in some sailor's arms, lulled by the singing and the rocking of the ship, because when I awoke, I was in my camp bed on deck, and it was daylight. Somebody must have carried me there, very gently.

Life on board ship was fun and as the ship's official mascot, I was allowed everywhere, although I noticed that the large sailor that the General had set to guard over me watched from a distance, so I would not fall overboard. You stayed in the cabin most of the time. You had your meals in the officers' mess, whilst I ate on deck with the crew. I think you needed to be alone to collect your thoughts, and I was perfectly happy chasing around the ship's decks all day.

But what were your thoughts, Mother, on the last day but one of our long journey home? Was "home" for you youth and laughter in the beautiful house on Tsakalof Street? Or was it your first great love, your first great sorrow? *Please do not wait for me my love, but please remember me...* And soon afterwards the telegram that he had died of consumption in a Swiss sanatorium. Was the pain blistering, scorching, like a burn? Did it leave a corner of your soul where nothing would ever grow again?

Was it the exaggerated gaiety of parties and balls, night after night, and the many many suitors, all too glamorous, too frivolous, too temporary, to last?

A friend and admirer, the writer George Theotokas, dedicated some humorous lines to you:

> *By many is she admired*
> *By diplomats and professors of law,*
> *By men of letters and generally*
> *By young men proficient in French*
> *And with great expectations...*

Was it the triumphant law-school finals, with your father so proud of his brilliant daughter? At the time, the same old admirer writes:

*She received her degree in Law*
*With the highest possible honours*
*And the unbounded praise of deans*
*and professors,*
*To acquire, as some said,*
*L'air d'une femme remarquable.*

Was it the trips abroad with your mother, to Paris, Salzburg, Vienna? Ease, security, gracious living. Was it enough to make you happy? Were there dark moments in the great, shady house, when you felt trapped by the complacent stability of unquestionable values? Why did you agree to marry my father, when you did not really love him? Was he somebody you could depend on, who was serious and responsible enough not to break your heart, but also adventurous enough to take you far away?

Were these your thoughts on the last day but one, of our long journey home? I will never know.

Towards evening a line of land on the horizon caused great excitement. "Crete! Crete!" the sailors cried. The first glimpse of Greece after so many years. Some even had tears in their eyes.

And as the line that was Crete was swallowed up in the darkness, some gathered in small groups talking in low voices, whilst others chose to remain alone. A match striking, the gleam of a cigarette, a cough, footsteps going away in the dark.

As we sailed into the night, I sat on my camp bed and you came and sat by me and held my hand. The sky was like a round glass dome above us, studded with a million stars, and it seemed as if outer space began at the edges of the sea. I believe that our silent thoughts and secret yearnings merged forever that last night and perhaps God in his glass dome knew, because certainly nobody else could have known anything at all.

## Chapter Seventeen

Next morning I stood by the railing on the top deck, as the ship ploughed through heavy masses of water. The sheer surfaces were like sheets of glass, cold and solid, and I was tempted to drop like a stone over the side... to descend gently and endlessly through opaque blue waters... for there was no floor to this sea...

> *Sea with your salty waters,*
> *Bring back my love to me.*

Someone called my name and shattered my trance-like state. As I brought my eyes up to the level of the horizon, the sun's refracted colours streaked the foreground and dimly, I could make out a fringe of land at the edge of the circling horizon, coming nearer now, an impression of dappled browns.

All my life there had been a word for this land, but no image. The journey from India had lasted too long, with too many impacts and impressions, too many stops and stages, so that in the jumble of new situations, new people and new places, I had lost all sense of sequence or purpose. Each new place had seemed like an uncharted and undeciphered world and in each I had unknowingly discovered new versions of myself, new versions of you.

In this long journey home there had been you and me. Always you and me in Delhi, in Karachi, in Basra, in Jerusalem, in Cairo, in Alexandria. Surely more than enough for a journey of three months, for a lifetime of eight years. Yet now we were nearing Greece. You and me. This is where we had been going all along, all this time, from the day we left Madras, a lifetime ago. This was supposed to be my country of origin, something I had never consciously perceived as true, considering my greekness one more paradox of my life in India.

My true origins had already been clearly revealed to me, in a recurring dream of a vast yellow grassland. There was room to run and no need to hide in that wondrous, infinitely ancient world. Whereas Greece, as I imagined it, was already limited by other people's descriptions and recollections that had no bearing on my own.

Yet the ship was carrying us closer and I knew, with growing apprehension, that contact with this unreal reality was now inevitable. Greece is a place, my mind said. There are people who live there and consider it their home, so that places like India are foreign to them. When they say something, they say it in Greek; even the small children don't have to be taught to speak Greek, as I had never been taught to speak English.

It was all incredibly confusing and my resentment grew. Why all these unnecessary problems when my life had been so settled in Madras? I had not asked for all these novelties and changes. Not at all. But it was too late to turn back now. I could already make out the houses on the seafront, white and square, and a bare, brown mountain behind. Then, as if my prayer for a reprieve was miraculously answered, the ship came to a dead stop. Mines, the sailors said. The Germans had left the sea outside the harbour of Piraeus riddled with mines.

A pilot came on board and gingerly we picked our way through the minefield, inch by inch. It was a strange relief, considering that we could have been blown sky high any moment, but it provided me with the time I needed to collect my wits. Two months later, we learnt that the Swedish ship that would have brought us from Alexandria hit a mine in the harbour and went down like a stone. So much for luck.

The soldiers and seamen stood motionless along the railings, as if the slightest movement or sound could detonate one of the mines in the sea. Feeling unwanted, I went below deck to find you. You were in the cabin, packing the last suitcase with the familiar deft, light movements of your hands. I watched you from the door. A small-boned woman, with a quick, expressive face, already marked and drawn beyond your thirty-six years. Your hair was turning grey and you were too thin and perhaps not very beautiful any more. But you were still everything to me.

So much had been taken from me in these last three months. Even the seasons of the year, the comforting tropical sequence of hot weather, cold weather, followed by hot weather again. Typically, some lines from a poem in Nanny's battered *Book of Irish Verse* came to my mind:

> *You have taken the east from me, you have taken the west from me,*
> *You have taken what is before me and what is behind me,*
> *You have taken the moon, you have taken the sun from me...*

But as long as you were here with me, Mother, nobody could ever take you from me.

You looked up with a startled expression. How fragile you had become.

"Is something wrong?"

"No. We've nearly arrived."

You were not aware of the danger we were

in. I purposefully safeguarded you from the knowledge. It was to become a lifelong habit.

"Wash your face and hands and put this dress on. I want you to look nice for your grandparents."

My grandparents. The click of knitting needles. A whiff of cigarette smoke. Long, long ago.

I thought that maybe after all there *is* a line from us to those that have gone before, an unbroken thread that cannot be seen but can be felt. Still, I could not be sure.

Always one for appearances, you were wearing an immaculate white dress and you had taken particular care with your hair and makeup. Obviously my appearance mattered too. You made me wear a white smocked dress and white shoes and socks. Any argument was out of the question, you seemed so preoccupied. My hair had grown so long that fixing it had become somewhat of a ritual. You untangled the knots and brushed it with a hundred brushstrokes, keeping time with the song Nanny used to sing in Khody a lifetime ago:

*He promised he'd buy me a bunch of blue ribbons,*
*He promised he'd buy me a bunch of blue ribbons,*
*He promised he'd buy me a bunch of blue ribbons,*
*To tie up my bonny brown hair...*

Then you twisted the side bits and braided each plait as smooth as silk, tying the ends with freshly ironed white satin ribbons.

"Let me have a look at you. Yes, you look very nice, but try not to get dirty before we arrive."

The ship was still creeping through the minefield, but we could see the houses lining the pier clearly now, through the porthole. I did not wish to be alone any more, we were too near, so I waited for you to pack your silver brushes into a small case and to inspect the cabin carefully to make sure that nothing was left behind. Then we went up on deck together.

We were almost in the port now, but the ship seemed to be taking ages to manoeuvre. We could see the people on the waterfront quite clearly and many little boats and barges milling around. The motion on the quay and in the boats seemed strange without the sound to accompany it, like watching a silent movie.

"Piraeus," you said softly and there were tears in your eyes. I took your hand. It seemed the only thing to do. What was in the word "Piraeus" to make you cry? Perhaps what might one day be in the word "Madras" to make me cry. But once again I wasn't sure if that was the reason. It seemed as if the older I grew, the less I understood what was in the minds of grown-up people, but it was time to make one last effort to get my facts together.

"Please tell me everybody's name again, Mother, so I will know who they all are."

On another occasion, you would have sensed and soothed my apprehension, but your own absorption and anxiety were so profound that you answered a bit vaguely.

"Don't worry. They're all very nice and they'll be so pleased to see you, such a big girl now. Greek people kiss a lot. You won't mind?"

"Will they all want to kiss me?"

"Your grandmother is sure to."

"But not all the others?"

"Perhaps not. Anyway there's nothing to worry about." The same slightly hackneyed phrase again. Surely you knew that words were not enough.

"Tell me quickly, before we stop."

I was not going to let you off so easily.

"Well, there's your grandfather, my father, and your grandmother, my mother. Then my brother, your Uncle Andreas, and his wife Ypatia, and their three children, Panagis, Eleni and Irene."

"Do they all live in the same house?"

"Yes."

There were other more essential questions I longed to ask, which all culminated in one basic uncertainty, "Will they accept me?" but the boat had docked by now and the noise was so deafening you couldn't have heard what I said anyway. The engines let out a last screech before being switched off, the funnel was still belching black smoke, the ship's bell was clanging and all around us people were shouting and screaming and charging about, pushing and shoving one another in their haste. I felt very bewildered and squeezed up close to you.

Then something extraordinary caught my attention. The porters who were yelling from the waterfront and catching the bales and bundles that the sailors were throwing down from the gangway were white men and were speaking Greek like everyone else. I was amazed. In all my life, I had never seen a white man perform any kind of manual labour. I pointed this out to you and again you laughed.

"We're in Europe now," you said.

Did you think desperately, "What am I going to do with this nonconforming, displaced, colonial child?" If you did, you kept your thoughts to yourself and together we descended the gangplank onto firm Greek soil.

## Chapter Eighteen

No one met us at the port. We had arrived a day too early. I looked to see if you showed any sign of concern or disappointment, but you seemed too preoccupied with organising our belongings and chasing the skinny, barefoot porters. When we were finally settled in a ramshackle taxi and heading towards Athens, you acknowledged the ultimate paradox of not being met after so many years away.

"They're expecting us tomorrow."

After that you didn't talk any more, but turned your gaze nervously on the street outside. You sat on the edge of the seat, clutching the back of the driver's seat, with your hands so taut, the knuckles had turned white. I sensed the tension in your posture and caught your anxiety. It was absurd not to be expected after so many years and I suspected that you were troubled too, by the emotions that would be provoked by our sudden arrival, a day too soon.

Once again, the timing was wrong. Why could we not have been expected today, so that our anticipation could be matched by theirs? And all these names, all these people I knew nothing of... they would be so interested in me... so curious... How could lives so divergent, so remote, affect each other so dramatically? I feared their familiarity that was just relationship and I feared my own ignorance of their characters and humours. Most of all I feared their affection that would seem misdirected towards a person of my likeness, whom they would profess to know, just because they knew who I was. It was all too confusing and of course my nervousness was making it more so.

For you it would be different. You would have to face the illusiveness of time and memory, the ordeal of comparison and change, perhaps both in yourself and in others whom you remembered differently. Naturally nostalgic, perhaps you really believed that the past could be resumed, whereas I feared that in the labyrinth of the last months I had lost my past forever. Neither of us spoke. It was better so, but suddenly my mind filled with the beautiful words that Marie had once recited to me in Jerusalem.

> *By the rivers of Babylon, we sat and wept, when we remembered Zion,*
> *How shall we sing the Lord's song in a strange land?*

I am in a strange land, my beloved Jewish friend Marie, whereas you are home in Zion.

Could it be that life is like a river, continually changing, continually moving, yet always a river? Now, before and after. I had no way of knowing.

We had left the waterfront and were driving up Syngrou Avenue, heading straight towards Athens. Squalid tenements lined the route, and dust-eaten shrubs. The midday July sun shone ruthlessly onto the flat ungainly buildings, erasing shades and contours. Buildings, plants and people seemed to be flattened into the ground by the weight of the heavy sunlit sky. And all this was Athens. The hurrying people, the mangy dogs, the squat buildings, the warped trees, and above all the blazing, violent sky.

"If I forget thee, O Jerusalem..."

I am dying of remembrance, Marie.

"We're nearly in Athens now," you said, suddenly breaking the silence. "Look up on the hill, that's the Parthenon, the most beautiful temple of the ancient world. Dedicated to the goddess Athena."

The white pillars sprouting from the rock laced the sky.

"Perhaps tomorrow..."

Tomorrow. Great God, I thought, how much would have happened and changed by then?

"The columns by the side of the road are what is left of the Temple of Olympian Zeus and that is the gateway built by the Roman Emperor Hadrian, who loved Athens."

How to tell you that I didn't care? Not about Hadrian or the ancient Greeks whose ancientness only made my newness more pronounced and painful.

The taxi driver asked over his shoulder, "How come she doesn't speak Greek?"

"She was born in India," you said. "She has only been to Greece once, when she was a baby."

"You must have been away many years."

"Twelve, all in all."

"Well, welcome home."

I felt sick. Already the excuses and explanations had begun, as if I was some kind of curiosity. You began a regular conversation with the taxi driver. He knew the family house and had been a supporter of my grandfather in his political days.

"Things were different then. Politicians cared about the country, about the people. Now they only care about themselves."

You glowed with pride, feeling, I suppose, that you still belonged to this past heroic world, whilst I felt miserably outcast, and for the hundredth time I questioned the sense of all this adventure and upheaval. I was tired of being constantly confronted with major decisions and I deeply resented the growing ambiguity and ambivalence of my own situation. I, who always went too far, longed to call a retreat.

What would I be doing in Madras now? A world away. Eating lunch with the other children under the giant banyan tree at Church Park School. The buzzing, sleepy atmosphere of a tropical afternoon, with the kites circling in the sky. And the one unforgettable time when the big boy called Clive actually smiled at me! After the lunch hour, the cool corridors and chalky classrooms. The rustle of the nuns' habits and the drone of children's voices:

> *Jack Spratt would eat no fat,*
> *His wife would eat no lean...*
>
> *Hark, hark the dogs do bark*
> *The beggars are coming to town...*

Lessons were lighter in the afternoon, mostly singing and sewing. The Indian children with their still, gentle eyes and strangely mobile fingers. The classroom scented by the flowers in their hair. I learnt to say "I love you" in Tamil to my best friend Radha, but my funny accent made her laugh like a tinkling bell. One afternoon we set fire to some dry leaves using a mirror and the rays of the sun and forgot to go into class.

Another time some naughty boys squirted juice from an orange into our eyes.

I am dying of remembrance, Radha.

At home, the tiles in the front hall were cool if you lay down on them... Chokra's duster went flop-flop every morning and Ayah's gums were all red from chewing betel-nut...

All this was India, where I belonged, where I was known, and where I knew myself.

I longed for what was familiar, named, remembered, understood, not new and undiscovered. If nostalgia means the "suffering of return" then that is definitely what I was suffering from.

"Here we are," the driver announced, as the taxi came to a lurching halt in front of an iron gate leading into a garden. It was three in the afternoon and there was nobody around. Your nervousness came welling back and the business of paying off the taxi and collecting our belongings in a stack on the pavement seemed interminable. I felt exposed and stupid and I looked warily around to make sure that no one was watching to witness the ridiculous fact that after so many years and so much trouble, there was nobody there to greet us and to welcome us home.

I stood there vacantly as you rang the bell. After what seemed like a long delay, the front door of the great house opened and a young girl with sloppy slippers and an apron round her hips came languidly down the walkway. She peered suspiciously through the grating without opening the gate.

"What is it?" she asked, eyeing the suitcases on the pavement.

I felt you grow tense at this surly reception and for a moment you seemed to lose all your presence of mind. You asked vaguely, "Is Madam in?"

"She's asleep," the maid said and turned to go.

What transpired later was that, during the German Occupation and the Greek Civil War, families with children and belongings had periodically appeared at the front gate, asking for temporary shelter and asylum. My grandparents had offered both, but a family that the maid had admitted was still comfortably ensconced on the third floor, with no intention of leaving. Unaware of this precedent, your exhaustion and the anxiety of weeks and months turned to fury. To be barred from your father's house was too much to bear.

"If it interests you at all," you shouted, "I happen to be Madam's daughter and this is her grandchild! We return after twelve years and I have to beg you to open the door of my father's house!"

It was all very dramatic and your voice rose to a pitch of hysteria that I had learnt to recognise in the last weeks. You were at the end of your tether. I laid a hand on your arm to soothe you, but I suddenly felt more relaxed, as if your indignation had dispelled my own fears and apprehension. If nobody opened the gate, we could just pick up our cases and go back to India!

The girl beyond the railing turned her startled, still uncomprehending eyes towards us throughout the outburst, and only when you paused for breath did a glimmer of faint recognition begin to dawn on her face.

"...But we were expecting you tomorrow..." she whispered almost soundlessly, and the poor, silly creature burst into tears as she fumbled with the latch of the gate.

A second before she managed to wrench open the gate, I asked you desperately, "When can we go back, Mother? When can we go back to India together?"

"Soon," you said, and I think you meant it.

But the soothsayer said, "Never."

## *The End*

# *Epilogue*

The soothsayer was right; we never went back to India together. But I went back to Delphi in 1973. I found this letter in your papers after you died. It is a kind of closure.

Delphi
Madras
January 14th, 1973

Dearest Mother,

I am writing to you from Delphi. We arrived a few hours ago and the house is so full of your presence that I had to write to you at once to tell you so.

India has welcomed me home and I am incredibly happy. I feel I have found the roots of my own strange identity, which never really tallied anywhere else – not in England, not in Greece. There *are* roots and one never fully recovers from being transplanted, but the traces of my footprints are still here.

I have dreamt of this return so long, to a world that is totally familiar. All the magic and the happiness of those first eight years that were scattered throughout my life have remained here, quite unchanged, not as a memory but as the reality of this moment too. I feel like the banyan tree that sends its shoots back into the earth and creates its own shade and its own strength. Perhaps this was the moment to touch base. These things never happen by chance.

Delphi has withstood time too. It is a bit disheveled and various occupants have left their mark in tasteless furniture and paintings. Amazingly enough however, some of your things are still here. The cane armchairs and the lamps are the same and someone has given them a fresh coat of paint. The house is shady and comforting and the smiling face of a white-haired Sam welcoming us at the door was incredibly moving, after so many years.

I am sleeping in Father's dressing-room, the

brightest room in the house. The garden has not many flowers, but the trees are lovely still. The old tamarin tree has not aged at all and the tree the servants planted when I was born has rather schizophrenically grown two trunks. But it has managed to get its head into the sun.

I am sorry you are not here. We should have been together. No time has passed at all. I love you.

D.

## *India Again*

Trace of my footprint everywhere
In stone, in sand, in dust.
Roots of the banyan tree
Renewed in strength and years.
If the dry leaves crumble
If the tree is callously cut down,
If the floods change the face of you,
Come and see my strangeness
And the life-line in my hand
And understand the extent of love
For I have never been away.

## *Wondertales*

Call memories wondertales
When kites trace circles still
In whitehot, burnt-out skies.
There are no spirits left
Just dust and painted visions,
Crimson and yellow for luck
And garish gay for sorrow.
Just man reborn in unnamed streets
With moisture and decay for life, for
air.
One time, one space inseparable.
Somewhere a touch of gold
And bangle sounds and whispers
of laughter,
Somewhere man tempted once again,
Yet graced again by the close-guarded
Knowledge of a deciphered dream.

# *Acknowledgements*

I should like to begin by thanking George and Marianna, who enjoyed the Indian stories when they were children, as their children have loved them too. They all insisted that I should write them down.

My husband Costa has lived with someone who invariably has a pen in her hand, like the scribe in Tutankhamen's tomb. I thank him for his forbearance.

My special thanks are due to all the people mentioned in the book, who have allowed me to take their names in vain. I hope that those who are no longer with us will not mind. With very few exceptions, names are authentic.

I am deeply grateful to my friend and editor, Lia Pavlidis Coulouris who battled with my handwriting and erratic punctuation, typed and retyped the manuscript and helped and advised me all the way. I could not have done it without her.

Equally to my friend, author and analytical psychotherapist Dr. Anthony Stevens who, as my first reader, understood more than I myself was aware of, and generously provided me with the encouragement I needed so much.

The same goes for another very wonderful friend and actor, Daniel Day-Lewis.

I thank my cousin Panagis Vourloumis for salvaging our grandfather's diaries, when the family house was pulled down. They have proved an inexhaustible source of information.

I wish to particularly express my appreciation to my publisher Louisa Zaousis and to all the charming and patient people at Oceanida, particularly Natasha Kouimountzi, Georgia Athanasiou, Demetris Papacostas and Takis Voreakos.

For the beautiful cover design, I am most grateful to the talented young artist Natalia Tsoukala.

Also I thank Evie Mela for tracing the lyrics of *Morgenrot* and Aristo Fridas for translating them from the German; Taddy Dyson Fordham for sending me Michael Malin's *Pagoda Tree* where the Greeks of Chinnapatnam are mentioned; Lily Alivizatos for the correspondence between her brother, the writer

George Theotokas and my mother; Alecos Pappas for the photograph of his father in Alexandria; and Sylvia Smith for discovering the source of *Lilliburlero*.

Also Leonidas Papademitriou for his computer skills with old and faded photographs.

Most of all I thank my mother for insisting that we do not forget, even after she had ceased to remember.

D. E.